# PocheCouleur

## In the same series :

* Also available in English

**Chief Editor :** Ahmed-Chaouki Rafif
**Iconography :** Lynne Thornton and ACR
**Assistant :** Marie-Pierre Kerbrat

© ACR PocheCouleur
© 1994, ACR Édition Internationale, Courbevoie (Paris)
(Art - Création - Réalisation)
© ADAGP et SPADEM, Paris, pour les artistes gérés par ces organismes
© Droits réservés
ISBN 2-86770-083-3
ISSN 1248-6981
N° d'éditeur : 1084/1
Dépôt légal : décembre 1994

Printed in France

# THE ORIENTALISTS
## Painter-Travellers

Lynne Thornton

**ACR Edition**

*PocheCouleur*

# INTRODUCTION

## *What is Orientalism ?*

The term Orientalist – meaning someone who is
knowledgeable about Oriental people, their languages, history,
customs, religions and literature – also applies to Western
painters of the Oriental world. For these artists – whose
numbers grew rapidly in the early nineteenth century – the
Orient meant first of all the Levant. It then included Egypt,
Syria, Lebanon, Palestine and the North African coast. Spain,
because of its Arab past, and Venice, because of its historical
connections with Constantinople, were viewed by many as the
gateway to the Orient. Only a few particularly adventurous
artist-travellers went to Arabia, Persia or India; as for the
countries in the Far East, they were virtually closed to
Westerners until the end of the nineteenth century.
There was no school of Orientalist painting; the pictures were
linked thematically rather than stylistically. Technique,
especially in the treatment of light and colour, evolved with
each decade, as the artist's experiences grew. There is a
century – as well as a whole world of discovery and better
understanding of the Orient – between the dark impasto of
Alexandre-Gabriel Decamps and the delicate watercolour washes
of Augustus Osborne Lamplough. But since many Orientalists
worked in the academic manner of their time (when the "well-
drawn" and the "well-painted" were highly admired), they
were virtually wiped off the slate of history when academicism
became unfashionable, ousted by the avant-garde. What had
fallen from favour was not the Orient, it was the old manner of
painting it. Only over the last two decades or so has
Orientalism, once known worldwide, begun to surge up again
into the consciousness of art historians, dealers and the public.
Paintings have reappeared in salerooms and galleries and
emerged from museum basements, while exhibitions have
again been held. Partly due to the general reassessment of the
last century – the ridiculous has again become the sublime – as
well as to a renewed esteem for technique, Orientalism has
again come back into favour. This is certainly not a passing
fashion, but a natural return, in the ever revolving cycle of

taste, of a justified appreciation of paintings that are marvellous invitations, visually, and through the imagination, to journeys to other lands and other times. Colourful, sunlit, strange, sanguinary, tender or instructive, they enchant and fascinate us as they did former generations. Each has its story to tell, of travel and adventure, sights and customs now changed forever, of the gradual lifting of the veils of myth and mystery in which the Orient had been shrouded and of the heady discoveries of exoticism by Westerners accustomed to the greyness of the northern industrialized cities.

## *The origins of Orientalism*

Many meeting points had, of course, existed between the Orient and the Occident before the nineteenth century, through a long history of mercantile, diplomatic and artistic relations. Examples include the Crusades, the close links between Venice and Turkey, Britain's establishment in India and France's use of commercial ports in the Levant. But, with the exception of European artists settled in Constantinople (described by A. Boppe in *Les Peintres du Bosphore au Dix-Huitième Siècle*) (Paris 1911, republished by A.C.R. Edition in 1989), Orientalism had been nearly exclusively decorative. Chinese, Japanese and Turkish culture and a general hotch-potch of "Eastern" styles influenced clothes, architecture and works of art. The storybook entitled *The Thousand and One Nights*, popularly known as *The Arabian Nights*, helped spread the vogue for exoticism, which still had no particular regard for exactitude.

The passion for Egyptology at the end of the eighteenth century, the founding of schools of Oriental studies and, most importantly, Napoleon Bonaparte's expedition to Egypt in 1798, brought the East into public view. The illustrated albums by the baron Dominique Vivant Denon of this survey of ancient and modern Egypt, as well as the Napoleonic history paintings in Oriental settings by the baron Gros, Anne-Louis Girodet-Trioson and others, laid the foundation for the Orientalist movement. The Greeks' struggle for independence from Turkish rule, the Romantics' espousal of their cause, the taking of Algiers by the French in 1830 and Delacroix's only too famous journey to Morocco in 1832 all helped open wide the doors to hundreds of artists who were to make the journey to the Orient. Travellers and stay-at-homes alike often relied

Edmond Dulac.
"Scharazade",
signed and dated
'11, L'Illustration,
special christmas
issue, 1911.

heavily on literary sources for their works. These were generally fiction, such as Lord Byron's Turkish epics, Thomas Moore's Indian romance *Lala Rookh,* Gustave Flaubert's *Salammbô*, Théophile Gautier's *Le Roman de la Momie* and Victor Hugo's *Les Orientales*. In addition, there were the recitals of their journeys, by influential writers and poets, including François-René de Chateaubriand, Alexandre Dumas père, Gérard de Nerval, Alphonse de Lamartine and Théophile Gautier.

## *Why did the Orientalists travel ?*

As the number of steamships and railway networks grew, so more and more painters joined the streams of people investigating, exploring, analyzing or just meandering in the East. These artists were primarily French and British; for other European countries, without major empires, the Orient was remote. The French artists were for the most part attached to military, scientific or diplomatic missions sent to countries around the Mediterranean basin and to Persia. (This was an area of great importance to France who was anxious to prevent Britain from extending her interests west of Afghanistan). The English, on the other hand, concentrated mainly on Egypt (the critical communication link in the overland route to their Indian Empire) and on Palestine. However, more English artists than of any other nationalities ventured alone into out-of-the-way, desolate places. The associations between the Bible and the Orient were very important, not only for such Victorian painters as David Wilkie, Holman Hunt and Frederick Goodall, but also for the Frenchmen James Tissot and Horace Vernet. They travelled primarily to find authentic backgrounds for their Biblical subjects, convinced that the gestures and attitudes of the people they saw were survivals from ancients times. The religious revivalism in Victorian England also made Biblical themes set in pharaonic Egypt popular, and Edward Poynter, Sir Lawrence Alma-Tadema and Edwin Long painted elaborate historical compositions remarkably like those found in early Hollywood films.

With time, the prestige of the artists who had insisted on seeing the Orient under different disguises faded once Europe had developed a real awareness of the interest and importance of Islamic culture and architecture. That Europeans began to lose their complacent sense of superiority was largely due to

6

the sensitivity and awareness of such travellers as the English Egyptologist Edward Lane and the painter John Frederick Lewis, who for years immersed themselves in native Cairene life. Incidentally, it is probable that many paintings of harem interiors were derived from accounts in Lane's authoritative, detailed book *Manners and Customs of Modern Egyptians* (London, 1836). It was virtually impossible for a male outsider to enter the harem quarters in a Muslim house (although there seem to have been a few exceptions). Lane was assisted by his sister, Sophia Poole, who had, she wrote, the opportunity of "seeing many things accessible only to a lady." When Orientalism became all the rage, even artists who had never visited the Orient were infected by the fever. The best known of these is the classicist Jean-Auguste-Dominique Ingres. As early as 1814, he had painted *Great Odalisque* (Musée du Louvre, Paris), followed by his famous works *Odalisque and Slave* (1839, Fogg Museum of Art, Cambridge, Massachusetts) and *Turkish Bath* (1862, Musée du Louvre, Paris).

The Crimean War of 1854-55 and the opening of the Suez Canal in 1869 again brought the Near East into the news. Not only were artists sent to report events, increasing numbers became interested in the actualities of everyday life in the Orient. But in pace with the swelling hordes of Thomas Cook tourists, clickclacking their Kodak cameras, European manners and costumes were being introduced into government circles in Cairo, and while Turkish ladies exchanged their traditional dress for crinolines by Worth, artists studiously avoided any hint of Europeanization. Most painted the more glamorous aspects, proud Nubian guards, falcon hunts and thoroughbred horses in immense spaces, gorgeously dressed women reclining in harems and market places full of busy, contented people. On the other hand, some began to show the harsher sides, the impoverished tribes of southern Algeria, blind beggars, the crumbling walls of tortuous streets.

## *The expansion of Orientalism*

By the 1870s, the British and French were no longer enjoying a virtual monopoly on Orientalist painting. After the Franco-Prussian war, Paris received an influx of European and American artists. Many were already well established in their own countries; others enrolled at the Académie Julian and at the Paris School of Fine Arts, especially under the direction of

Jean-Léon Gérôme, himself a great traveller. They gravitated to Paris rather than to the Royal Academy School in London, which not only lacked any system of ateliers led by an established master as in France, but had no structure of rewards, nor any prospects of State employment for even the most gifted student. Indeed, the British painters were never so well known as their continental counterparts, although they took part in the Paris Universal Exhibitions in 1855, 1867, 1878, 1889 and 1900. This was perhaps because of an inborn insularity or because they found the French technical mastery admirable but lacking in warmth.

Not all the Orientalists were based in London or Paris. The Austrian Leopold Carl Müller encouraged his fellow Viennese to paint in Egypt, and in Italy the Spaniard Mariano Fortuny y Marsal was behind an entirely new interest in the Orient. Swiss, German, Belgian and Scandinavian artists began to paint abroad and exhibit in their home towns. In Turkey, Osman Hamdy Bey founded a School of Fine Arts in Constantinople and launched the short-lived Stamboul Salons. This was the first time that Orientals had painted in oils in the Western tradition, besides the Persian Qajar artists, although human figures already existed in the celebrated Turkish, Persian and Indian miniatures.

### *Travelling in the Orient*

For many painters, particularly the early travellers, such as Alexandre-Gabriel Decamps, Eugène Delacroix and Théodore Chassériau, one journey sufficed. Their paintings were, for the rest of their lives, nourished by haunting memories of this contact with the Orient. For the most part, however, painters were bitten with the travel-bug. There was of course a certain element of "gathering" exotic subjects for their paintings – and their public – as though they were chasing brightly coloured butterflies. But very often it was a real sense of excitement and adventure that drew them back again and again. In Egypt, travelling was relatively organized and easy – studios could even be found in Cairo – where, as in Alexandria, Constantinople, and Algiers, the European community had comfortably settled itself. Once out on their own, however, it was very necessary for Europeans to wear Oriental dress. Although this was really for safety reasons, it did add to the romance. David Roberts, who crossed the Sinai desert with twenty-one camels and as many servants, wrote that he was "so completely transmogrified in appearance that my dear old mother would never know me." By the 1870s, handbooks for tourists discouraged the wearing of Oriental clothes unless one spoke Arabic, as it would look ridiculous. But it must have been an ordeal to paint in torrid heat, wearing a hard collar and tie, such as those in which Leopold Carl Müller was photographed during one of his trips to Cairo. Strange headdresses were devised to keep out the sun; the eccentric Edward Lear sported a "straw hat with a brim as large as a cart-wheel with a white calico cover."

Although many stayed abroad for years, or returned on numerous occasions, others "did" countries at an impossible

pace. Richard Dadd and his patron, Sir Thomas Phillips, made a lightning tour through Asia Minor to Beirut and Jerusalem, only to set out the following day for Jordan and the Dead Sea. The stages were long, the pace unrelenting and the conditions exhausting. Dadd, Patricia Allderidge reports, particularly lamented that their mode of travel left little opportunity to sketch, since the light was nearly always gone by the time they stopped and "a body can't very well sketch on horseback." It is easy to laugh at the idea of these Europeans careering round the interesting "spots," bouncing around on camels, cluttering themselves up with paraphernalia: photographic and

Edmund Berninger. *Caravan*, oil on canvas, signed, 35 x 59 in (89 x 150 cm). Courtesy of the Mathaf Gallery, London.

painting equipment, canteens of silver and parasols; Arthur Melville even took his Scottish plaid and Bible. Plum pudding and mulled wine at Christmas, turbans slipping across their burnt, heated faces, losing battles with their recalcitrant bumpy and humpy mounts... ridiculous, perhaps. But then read the magical travel journals of Berchère, Flandin, Roberts, Lear. Their appreciation and admiration for the beauty of the lands they saw were unfeigned, and their courage in the face of hardship, danger and frequent illnesses admirable.

## *Studio painting at home*

Painting on the spot usually caused difficulties. The quite natural hostility of local populations towards European artists, particularly in holy or remote places, attacks by bandits, the heat, which made oil paints run, clustering flies and the jostling, curious crowds in busy streets made it all extremely trying. Travellers would therefore for the most part dash off quick sketches in pencil, ink or watercolour. These, free and uninhibited by the restraints of building up a complex composition, are often remarkable. Watercolour, used brilliantly by Delacroix, Roberts and Lear for their studies was, for many Orientalists, such as John Frederick Lewis, Carl Haag, Charles Robertson, Mariano Fortuny y Marsal and the Italians, an alternative to oils. Watercolour had not always been thought suitable for finished works, however. A particularly English art (the Watercolour Society was founded in 1804), it was considered in France at the beginning of the nineteenth century as being a minor technique, suitable for use only as a pastime for well-born ladies and young girls. However, when the raising of the blockade after the Napoleonic wars allowed artists to go freely between France and England, it was adopted by many continentals. The introduction of photography is widely assumed to have put the academic artists' noses out of joint, since it was too close to their realistic painting for them to have any further reason to exist. In fact, the academics – and these of course included many Orientalists – were extremely interested in this new phenomenon and frequently used photographs as aide-mémoires. As early as 1839, Horace Vernet and Frédéric Goupil-Fresquet were taking daguerreotypes in Egypt and Jerusalem and many later artists took their own photographs or were accompanied on their travels by a technician. It was also possible to buy prints on the spot, of scenery, architecture and local types. The best known, and some of the most original, were by Félix Bonfils who specialized in the Near East. Those artists who, preferring not to work in premises abroad, returned to Europe to produce their paintings, made extensive use of Islamic works of art and Oriental costumes as studio props. As early as 1824, Jules-Robert Auguste had already amassed a large collection, while Théodore Chassériau completely transformed his premises into a riotous display of colour, as described by Théophile Gautier: "Yataghans, kandjars, Persian daggers, Circassian pistols, Arabian rifles, ancient Damascened blades adorned with nielloed Koranic

inscriptions, silver- and coral-decorated firearms – all these beguiling barbaric treasures were arranged like trophies on the walls. Gandouras, haiks, burnous, caftans, and silver- and gold-embroidered jackets were draped casually here and there..." Towards the end of the century, the successful, affluent artists in Paris, who lived for the most part in the newly-built area around the Parc Monceau, recreated astonishing worlds of make-believe. The military painters were surrounded by arms, armour and stuffed horses, the historical painters by Henri IV

A.E. Duranton.
*The Goupil Family's Home,*
oil on canvas,
signed,
25.25 x 35.75 in
(64 x 91 cm).
Private collection.

buffets, figured velvets and feathered musketeers hats, the Orientalists by carpets, textiles and works of art. But since the artists were not always aware of the dates or origins of their finds, this sometimes led to anachronisms. Even such a carefully accurate artist as Jean-Léon Gérôme would introduce a helmet or a gun from a different period or country into the same picture. Curiously enough, this taste for extravagant decors was not nearly so common in England. However, when John Frederick Lewis returned home from Egypt in 1851, he brought back dresses, Bedouin cloaks, musical instruments and arms. Carl Haag decorated his Hampstead home in the Oriental manner, while Frederick, Lord Leighton, a Royal Academician who made three journeys to the East, was so fascinated by the Arab world that he altered his Kensington house (now a museum) to incorporate an Arab hall. He also built up a considerable collection of Islamic ceramics and textiles, helped by the explorer Richard Burton. Frederick Goodall even went so far as to have local sheep and goats shipped home to ensure authenticity in his Biblical scenes of rural life. In the United States, too, there was a vogue for Oriental decors, due in part to the success of the Orientalist paintings by the Americans Edwin Lord Weeks and Frederick Arthur Bridgman, as well as to Gérôme's popularity amongst American collectors.

## *Exhibitions, collectors and museums*

Artists found markets for their work abroad; Prosper Marilhat obtained commissions in Alexandria and Jules Laurens was badgered by Persian notables for their portraits in Teheran. There was a ready sale, too, for paintings amongst the English wintering in Egypt. But it was above all through the Royal Academy in London and the Paris Salon that artists found purchasers, particularly during the first three-quarters of the nineteenth century, when these institutions dominated the art scene. In the eighteenth century, the enjoyment of art and the exercise of patronage had been the privileges of the court and aristocracy. By the nineteenth century, the industrial revolution had created a new, powerfully wealthy middle class which no longer commissioned artists to paint what it wished, but bought finished works. Although it is true that Alexandre-Gabriel Decamps, Horace Vernet and Prosper Marilhat were particularly favoured by the Marquess of Hertford and the duc d'Aumale, the work of most of the Orientalists was purchased by manufacturers, shipowners and financiers, particularly those from the English Midlands and North America. Unlike the lordly patrons of the previous century, whose taste had been formed by Old Masters hanging in ancestral homes or seen in Italy on the Grand Tour, these new buyers, often from humble origins, preferred to buy modern painting. Not only that, Orientalism, with its scenes of opulence, exoticism, savagery and sensuality, offered them an exciting escape from the convention-bound society in which toil and duty were prized virtues. It was, however, more reassuring to select pictures that had been sanctified by official acceptance either by the Royal Academy or the Salon. Often, an exhibited painting was so much in demand that the artist was obliged to paint replicas for the disappointed would-be purchaser. However, not all the

pictures were bought by the collectors themselves. They were often acquired on the advice of Ernest Gambart in London and Adolphe Goupil in Paris. These influential dealers would also sell engraved reproductions of paintings that had passed through their hands, thus popularizing artists among people who could not afford to own an original. Many paintings eventually found their way to English and American museums. A typical example is the remarkable and varied collection formed by the businessmen William T. Walters and his son Henry, now housed in the Walters Art Gallery in Baltimore,

Jean-Léon Gérôme. *Prayer on the Housetops*, oil on panel, signed, 19.75 x 32 in (49.9 x 81.2 cm). Kunsthalle, Hamburg.

Maryland. A catalogue of the nineteenth-century paintings has been published by the museum's associate director, William R. Johnston.

In France, the system of prizes, culminating in the coveted Prix de Rome, generally led to commissions from the State, or, during the monarchy, the court. Delacroix, for instance, although one of the great artistic innovators of the period, received both official and academic recognition. Some Orientalists, however, by setting out on their travels when very young, made their names without having to take the conventional road to success. As artists could often command enormous sums of money, the French State could not always afford to buy their work, which explains in part the dearth of important Orientalist pictures in French provincial museums today. The Musée du Louvre, however, received many donations and the Musée du Luxembourg owned interesting examples. The holdings of this Paris museum of living artists, dispersed in 1939 amongst other museums, ministries and official institutions, have now been reunited in the Musée d'Orsay in Paris.

By the 1880s, the Orientalists were exhibiting their paintings in European and American cities other than London and Paris. Both the Royal Academy and the Salon, by now known as the Salon de la Société des Artistes Français, had become Gargantuan extravaganzas. In London, some five thousand artists submitted as many as twelve thousand works for selection, while in France, five thousand or so paintings, drawings and sculptures were shown every year. There had been for some time, all the same, alternative places to exhibit in London, including the New Watercolour Society, the Grosvenor Gallery, the Society of British Artists and the British Institution. In Paris, a break-away Salon was founded in 1890, the Salon de la Société Nationale des Beaux-Arts, followed by many of the older Orientalists as well as the up-and-coming generation.

## *Orientalism's new lease of life*

Throughout the century, Orientalism had been alternatively acclaimed or rejected by critics and the public as each generation replaced overworked themes with new pictorial images and techniques. By the turn of the century, it seems to have come to an end as an important artistic movement, except for Belgium (which governed the Congo) and for France, with her widespread overseas possessions. Sarah Searight, in her fascinating and well-informed book *The British in the Middle East* (1969), suggests moreover that the romantic attachment of the British in that area did not survive their acquiring political responsabilities. French Orientalism (and this includes foreigners living in France) took on a new lease of life with the creation of the Société des Peintres Orientalistes Français in 1893. Under the presidency of Léonce Bénédite, chief curator of the Musée du Luxembourg, its aim was to "further the state of knowledge concerning the countries and native races of the Near and Middle East, as well as of the Far East, to foster a critical approach to the study of their ancient arts and civilizations and to give impetus to a revival of interest in their

Rudolf Ernst. *The Dignitary,* oil on panel, signed, 28.25 x 36.25 in (72 x 92 cm). Courtesy of Alain Lesieutre, Paris.

local industries." Members of the society, which held retrospective exhibitions of the works of earlier Orientalists, included Emile Bernard, Charles Cottet, Etienne Dinet, Paul Leroy and the Impressionists Albert Lebourg and Auguste Renoir, both of whom had spent time in Algeria.

It is significant that the society's inaugural show took place in connection with one of the first Islamic art exhibitions, held in the Grand Palais in 1893. Although Islamic art had influenced ceramics and glass in Europe from the 1870s, collectors had preferred Japanese and Chinese art. By the 1890s, however, Islamic art began to be seriously studied by an elite circle of connoisseurs with whom certain later Orientalists were closely connected. It was through Etienne Dinet that one of the great experts, Gaston Migeon, was introduced to the subject. Dinet's editor, Henri Piazza, was an early collector of miniatures, and Albert Aublet, who painted for years in Tunisia, acquired textiles, ceramics, manuscripts and miniatures. These were no longer bought with an eye merely to form and colour, but were chosen knowingly and selectively. In addition, Islamic art would be having an enormous impact on early twentieth-century painters, including Auguste Macke, Wassily Kandinsky, Henri Matisse and Paul Klee; after decades of playing the role of a decorative accessory in pictures, it would instead be laying the base for abstract painting. From the 1890s to 1940, some two thousand French painters travelled overseas, mainly in the French possessions from the West Indies and the Pacific islands to northern and central Africa and Indochina. While most of these Orientalists adopted a more modern manner of painting, some – notably Ludwig Deutsch, Rudolf Ernst and Etienne Dinet – continued in the academic tradition throughout the 1920s.

### *Research on the Orientalists and hints to collectors*

Gathering information about the Orientalists is a curious business. In many cases, no monographs were published during their lifetimes even on relatively well-known painters, and it is only due to recent research that we now know more about their lives. In many cases, copious articles were written during the artist's lifetime, but these were often misleading or erroneous, either because the writers did not take the trouble to check, or because the artist was interviewed at the end of his life, when his memory was hazy. The titles given at the time to paintings (and faithfully recorded in this book whenever known), often had misspelt place names or awkward transliterations. Not only that, the titles themselves often differed depending on the source. Works were not necessarily painted the year in which they were exhibited (some artists showing pictures as much as a decade later). Unless a picture is well-recorded or dated, it is virtually impossible to be entirely precise. The book on French nineteenth-century Orientalism by Jean Alazard, first curator of the Algiers museum of Fine Arts, published in 1930, is a model of accuracy. However, he treats only the great names of the movement at length, devoting considerable space to Albert

Lebourg and Auguste Renoir, perhaps natural for a man who was drawn more to the Impressionnists than to the academics. Artists' diaries and journals, when they exist, are of course invaluable sources of information, although in some cases (the memoirs of Georges Clairin, for instance) they are vague about dates and lack the information we would most like to know. Exhibition catalogues had introductions that were either too terse, or too verbal and flowery, to be of much help. Auction catalogues of artists' studios, particularly in France, often turn up trumps, however, when they are prefaced by a friend or a well-known critic who gave a much-needed résumé of the artist's life. It is interesting to note, however, that due to the extraordinarily widespread interest in the Orientalists over the last few years, students from Paris, Aix-en-Provence, Hamburg, Zurich, Tunis, North Carolina and New York, to mention only a few places, are doing research for university theses. These deal with single artists, their own national schools of painting or different aspects of English and French Orientalism.

It is a general rule that artists who were famous in their time reappear at the top of the list when there is a renewal of interest in a subject, for reputations were rarely won without a good reason. But to be blinded by a signature is an error; there can be mediocre paintings in every artist's œuvre. On the other hand, one can find many remarkable pictures by artists whose names are not even listed in the art dictionaries. This does not mean that the hundreds of hangers-on, who followed in the wake of a then fashionable movement, with their wobbly camels, chocolate-box sunsets and cardboard palm-trees, are of any interest. Yet there are beautiful and well-painted pictures by practically unknown artists. The latter were perhaps overlooked by critics, hardly ever exhibited, painted few pictures or merely disdained the medals and honours that automatically brought an artist's name into the limelight.

# Albert
## AUBLET

**Paris 1851-Paris 1938**
*French School*

*L*ike many artists of his time, Albert Aublet painted a wide range of subjects: historical and religious scenes, interiors, the seaside town of Tréport, elegant ladies and coy nudes. He was also an Orientalist, whose early, academic works in the manner of his professor, Jean-Léon Gérôme, were very different in feeling to those painted in Tunisia after 1900.

Aublet was noticed by the critic Edmond About at his first Salon in 1873, when his painting, *Interior of Butcher's Shop, Tréport* was bought by Alexandre Dumas fils. He was soon being sought after by such collectors as Georges de Porto-Riche, the Prince Regent of Bavaria, Henri Béraldi and the Vanderbilts.

In 1881, Aublet made the first of his journeys to the Eastern world, visiting Constantinople and Brusa, perhaps in the company of Gérôme, who was in Turkey that year. During this trip, he went to Scutari, a quarter of Asiatic Constantinople which, with Brusa, was the main centre of the howling dervishes, the Rūfa'i, an order founded in the twelfth century. In Aublet's painting illustrated here, the sheikh or master walks gingerly over the backs of a row of prostrate boys inside a tekke, or dervish convent. The original subtitle for this picture, exhibited at the 1882 Salon, was *Treading on Children's Bodies to Ensure Them Allah's Protection.* It seems more likely, however, that it concerns either an initiatory ceremony – the mūrids, or neophytes, lie on a bearskin, symbol of authority – or else a healing ceremony. Very similar scenes, described as the healing of the sick by the Rūfa'i of Scutari, can be seen both in an English engraving of the period and in a painting by an Italian artist living in Constantinople, Fausto Zonaro. The Rūfa'i were incidentally, said to have the faculty of miraculously curing their wounds inflicted on themselves during religious frenzies.

Two years later, in 1883, Aublet travelled through Spain to Algiers with Gérôme and Alberto Pasini, an Italian Orientalist. Before changing from the Artistes Français to the Société Nationale des Beaux-Arts, a breakaway Salon founded in 1890, he showed a charming picture entitled *Gathering Around a Score by Massenet*, in which the composers Jules Massenet, Vincent d'Indy and Claude Debussy are grouped around a piano by the side of fashionable women.

Aublet was friends with many members of the musical, literary and artistic worlds, whom be used to entertain in his Neuilly studio. This was decorated in the Oriental style. Aublet had first visited Tunis around 1901 and, in 1904, he painted the portrait of the bey. The following year, having decided to settle there, he purchased a superb old palace,

exhibited in many cities, from Munich, Madrid and Berlin to Cairo, Moscow, Chicago and Buenos Aires. He sent his landscapes and bold close-up portraits of Tunisians to the Salon des Peintres Orientalistes Français and the Colonial Exhibitions in Marseilles and Paris in 1906, 1922 and 1931.

Dâr ben Abd-Allah, now a museum of local arts and crafts. He spent a large part of each year in North Africa and became president of the first artistic salon, the Société des Artistes de Tunis. Aublet

*Ceremony of the Howling Dervishes of Scutari,* oil on canvas, signed and dated 1882, 43.75 x 57.50 in (111 x 146.3 cm). Private collection.

# Gustav
## BAUERNFEIND

**Sulz-am-Neckar 1848-Jerusalem 1904**
*German School*

*The Gate of the Great Mosque, Damascus*,
oil on panel, signed, inscribed Damaskus
and dated Munchen 1891, 43 x 32.75 in
(109.2 x 83.2 cm). Courtesy of the Mathaf
Gallery, London.

*L*ittle had been published about
Gustav Bauernfeind's life and travels
until Hugo Schmid's study of 1980,
although his powerful, large
paintings of Jerusalem, Jaffa and
Damascus are very much sought
after today by collectors.
He was one of five surviving
children born to the second wife
of Johann Baptist Bauernfeind. His
father, a chemist, had been converted
to Catholicism, something that was
most unusual for the times. The
latter took an active part in the 1848
German revolution, for which he was
imprisoned and, in 1853, left Sulz
with his family to settle in Stuttgart.
During the 1860s, Gustav
Bauernfeind became a brilliant
student of architecture. He began to
draw during a journey to
Switzerland, where he had gone after
winning a prize; the resultant
topographical and architectural
studies were later reproduced by
wood engravings. In 1873, he
received a publisher's commission to
draw similar views, this time in
Italy. These were so successful that
he was soon much in demand
and made further journeys for other
publishers. Already an excellent
draughtsman and a keen observer
of detail, he became such a good
colourist that his paintings were
eagerly bought by collectors.
After winning a competition for a
large watercolour of the Bayreuth
opera house, commissioned by
Ludwig II, he was able to travel
to Egypt, Syria and Palestine,
venturing as far as Jerusalem. One of
the paintings from this 1880 trip,
entitled *Ruins of the Temple of
Baalbek*, was purchased by the Neue
Pinakothek in Munich. In 1885,
Bauernfeind stayed with one of his

sisters and her husband in Beirut, where he made many sketches of people, buildings, landscapes and camels. He began to exhibit his pictures in Munich, Nuremberg and Vienna, making a speciality of views of Jerusalem, Damascus and Jaffa, which he visited again on a number of occasions. These last two cities were rarely painted by artists. Only relatively recently had European consuls been allowed into the holy city of Damascus, an annual assembly point for thousands of hajj pilgrims to Mecca. Indeed, until about 1830, it was so notorious for its fanaticism that no one dressed as a European would go near it. As for Jaffa, not only was it often in fever quarantine, but most travellers were too eager to reach Jerusalem to stay there long. It was difficult, even dangerous, for Bauernfeind to work; he could not go unnoticed, with his photographic equipment and materials for watercolour painting. A number of his watercolours from this period, together with others painted in Jerusalem, are now in the Staatliche Graphische Sammlung, Munich.

Bauernfeind did not try to glamourize the cities, but showed them with narrow streets and crumbling walls and houses. However, he did paint a number of grandiose pictures of the courtyard of the Great Mosque of the Omayyads in Damascus, once considered one of the wonders of the world, but badly damaged by fire in 1893. In another of his paintings, similar in composition and lighting, *At the Entrance to the Temple Mount, Jerusalem*, the Dome of the Rock is glimpsed through the great doorway. Others of his oils, usually painted in Munich from sketches and photographs, include *Jaffa Street Scene, Gate of the Great Mosque in Damascus* and *Bethlehem*.

In 1898, with his family, Bauernfeind settled in Jerusalem where, after returning from a tiring trip to Beirut (he had a weak heart), he died in 1904.

*Street Scene in Jerusalem*, oil on canvas, signed and inscribed Jerusalem, 43 x 33 in (109.2 x 84 cm). Private collection.

# Léon
# BELLY

**Saint-Omer 1827-Paris 1877**
*French School*

Belly's first journey to the Near East
was in 1850, when he and another
painter, Léon Loysel, accompanied a
scientific mission to study the local
historical geography, led by
L.F. Caignard de Saulcy. They
skirted the Dead Sea, and in April
the following year, Belly and Loysel
went north to Beirut before visiting
Cairo and Alexandria. Belly's
pictures of this trip, such as the
classical ruins of Baalbek and the
curious olive trees at Nabi Jonas,

*L*éon Belly is known above all for
his imposing painting entitled
*Pilgrims going to Mecca,* considered
one of the masterpieces of Orientalist
painting. Purchased by the French
State in 1861, hung in the Musée du
Luxembourg until 1881, and now in
the Musée d'Orsay, Paris, it saved
Belly's name from oblivion during
the years when other nineteenth-
century artists were in limbo, victims
of changing taste in art. His pictures
remained in the hands of friends and
collectors who bought them at the
1878 studio sale, or were kept by his
widow and children. Despite
successive donations by the family
to museums in Switzerland and
France (Hôtel Sandelin in Saint-
Omer owns the largest collection), it
is only been in the last fifteen years
that his other works have been
rediscovered and appreciated. From
a moneyed family, Belly was
brought up by his mother, his father
having died in 1828. After being
admitted to the Polytechnic School,
he chose painting as a career,
spending a short time in Picot's
atelier. But it was primarily through
his contacts and friendship with the
Barbizon painters that he received
his artistic training.

between Beirut and Sidon, show a
certain influence of Prosper Marilhat
in both colouring and treatment.
Back in France, Belly painted the
Fontainebleau forest and spent an
active social life with his own
musical evenings and gatherings
with the artistic and literary circle

that had formed around the painter Jules Laurens. His first Salon in 1853 included pictures of the outskirts of Beirut and Cairo. At the Paris 1855 Universal Exhibition, however, he showed French landscapes and the portrait of the great Italian exile Daniel Manin. Belly returned to the Eastern world in October 1855, this time to Egypt, where he stayed in the palace of Soliman Pasha in Old Cairo. In the following spring, he visited the Sinai strange, almost fantastic atmosphere depending only on the rise and fall of the arid ground. "The colours and contours of the landscape are breathtakingly beautiful," he wrote to his mother. "There are no words to describe the gorgeous colourings, the stunning harmony of an almost violet sky above the sand tinged with mingled purple and gold against a turquoise sea." Two other canvases, now in the Musée National des Arts d'Afrique et d'Océanie in Paris, *The*

desert with his friend Narcisse Berchère; the two artists often painted the same views. Berchère was to buy *Banks of the Nile*, shown at the London Universal Exhibition in 1862, in Belly's studio sale. Belly's desert landscapes are remarkable, empty of figures, their

*The Gazelle Hunt*, oil on canvas, signed and dated 1857, 29.25 x 57.50 in (74.5 x 146 cm). Private collection.

*Libyan Desert* and *The Dead Sea* (Belly's most famous painting after *Pilgrims*), also impart a striking and disturbing appearance to the desolateness of these regions. With Edouard Imer, whom he had met in Cairo, Gérôme, Berchère and Bartholdi, Belly explored the Nile in July to October 1856, painting a series of small pictures, either from the boat on which they were travelling, or from the water's edge. They show his strong interest in colour harmonies and appreciation of light values. He also made naturalistic studies of camels and buffaloes and oil sketches of figures in bold strokes, where mass and forceful presence prevail over any anecdotal detail. Already struck on a previous visit by the nobility of the gestures made by the Egyptian fellah women, he made further studies for a picture exhibited in 1863, his first with figures. Belly returned once more to Egypt, in 1857, when Louis Mouchot became his pupil. After his marriage in 1862, Belly gave up any ideas of more great journeys, but soon won a solid reputation as an Orientalist painter. The 1861 Salon, with views of the Near East and, above all, *Pilgrims,* was a personal triumph. Although the great importance of the latter was the

originality of its lighting, Belly intended this impressive painting to have a greater signification than a mere recording of this religious event, when the sacred carpet, the *mahmal,* was carried with the pilgrims to Mecca. As P. Wintrebert points out in his 1974 thesis on Belly, the Holy Family can be seen to the left: Belly believed that there was a universal religion and one faith in the same God.

24

Although he continued to exhibit successfully at the Paris Salons during the next few years (*The Sirens* was bought by the State in 1867), by 1874, he failed to find any purchasers for his work. He spent much of his time in his château of Montboulan and although temporarily paralysed, soon recovered enough to work again. He died of apoplexy in his Paris home in 1877.

*Pilgrims Going to Mecca,* oil on canvas, signed and dated 1861, 63.25 x 95.25 in (161 x 242 cm). Musée d'Orsay, Paris.

# BENJAMIN-CONSTANT

## Paris 1845-Paris 1902
### *French School*

*B*enjamin-Constant's Paris studio, in Pigalle, was filled with objects brought back from his visits to Spain and Morocco. Carpets were hung on the walls, textiles swagged over balconies, plump, embroidered cushions lay on divans, providing the artist with an exotic background for his paintings, executed for over a decade following his journey. Of a Languedoc family, descended from the politician Benjamin Constant de Rebecque, Jean-Joseph Benjamin Constant (called Benjamin-Constant) spent his youth in Toulouse. There

he studied at the art school before enrolling at the Paris School of Fine Arts under the direction of Alexandre Cabanel. He made his Salon debut in 1869 with *Hamlet and the King*.

After fighting in the Franco-Prussian war in 1870, he did not resume his studies. Instead, he left for Spain, visiting Madrid, Toledo, Córdoba and Granada (where he met Mariano Fortuny y Marsal). The Mudejar architecture of Granada was used later in his large oil, *Aftermath of a Victory at the Alhambra: Moorish*

*Arabs in an Interior,* oil on canvas, signed,
22 x 33 in (56 x 84 cm). Private collection.

*Spain, Fourteenth Century* (Salon of 1882, Montreal Museum of Art), in which female captives and other spoils are shown being inspected by a ruler and his retinue.

Following in the footsteps of Fortuny, Henri Regnault and Georges Clairin, he crossed the Straits of Gibraltar to Morocco, in the company of Charles Tissot. The diplomat left shortly afterwards for Fez with Clairin, while Benjamin-Constant, who had intented to stay for only a month, lingered for, it seems, two years.

The first of his paintings resulting from this sojourn was *Riff Women, Morocco*, shown at the 1873 Salon. This was followed by a series of sumptuous Oriental scenes, characterized by richness of colour and lavish detail. Women were the subject of many of these, such as *Moroccan Harem*, *The Sharifas* (Musée des Beaux-Arts, Carcassonne), *The Emir's Favourites* and *Evening on the Terraces, Morocco*. The latter, now in the Montreal Museun of Art, became well-known through photographic reproductions. Others, often historical scenes, were more dramatic and violent: the monumental *Mohammed II Entering Constantinople the 29th May 1453* (Musée des Augustins, Toulouse), *The Last Rebels* (ex-Musée du Luxembourg, whereabouts unknown) and *Sherif Meting Out Justice* (Musée d'Orsay, Paris, on loan to the Musée de Lunéville). Benjamin-Constant's taste for opulence and pomp led him to be interested in other regions and epochs. His

*Saracen Reclining on a Divan,* oil on panel, signed, 9.25 x 12.50 in (23.5 x 32 cm). Courtesy of the Gallery Keops, Geneva.

biblical and Byzantine figures included *Judith, Herodias, Theodora* and a colossal *Justinian.* But when this last picture failed to win him a gold medal at the 1886 Salon, he gradually abandoned his Orientalist and historical phase.

He replaced his aging master, Cabanel, at the Paris School of Fine Arts in 1883, and five years later was appointed to succeed Gustave Boulanger at the Académie Julian, the haven for foreign art students in

1887-88, where he received portrait commissions from a number of prosperous businessmen. His portraits were as successful in England, where his distinguished sitters included Queen Victoria, Queen Alexandra and Lord Dufferin and Ava. A member of the Institut in 1893, he devoted his time during the last few years of the century to decorating public buildings in Paris, including the Sorbonne and the Opéra-Comique.

Paris. Here, he influenced the development of many American and Canadian painters of that period, while his own work was eagerly sought after by nouveau riche collectors from North America. This was in part due to the promotional activities of dealers, particularly Goupil et Cie and their successors, Boussod, Valadon et Cie. This popularity among Americans encouraged him to visit New York in

*The Pet Leopard,* oil on panel, signed and dated 1880, 31.50 x 47.25 in (80 x 120 cm). Private collection.

*Harem Women,* oil on panel, signed, 40.50 x 32.25 in (126 x 82 cm). Private collection.

# Narcisse
# BERCHÈRE

### Étampes 1819-Asnières 1891
*French School*

$A$lthough Narcisse Berchère was never a celebrity, he nevertheless has his place in the history of Orientalism, as much for his deep attachment to the desert as for his paintings.

A pupil of Renoux and then of Rémon at the School of Fine Arts in Paris, he soon left, after failing to win the Grand Prix de Rome. He spent several years travelling around France. His early landscapes, in sober colours, were influenced by Théodore Rousseau, Paul Huet and Jules Dupré, who were to form the Barbizon school of open-air painting. As he went further south, to Provence, the Balearic Isles and Spain, his palette became lighter and richer. Between 1849 and 1850, he visited Egypt, Asia Minor, the Greek archipelago and Venice, sending his paintings to the Salon and the Paris Universal Exhibition of 1855, when be received his first official award. He began to engrave his own work, having already made two eaux-fortes, *King Lear* and *Hamlet*, in 1854, from drawings by the Symbolist painter Gustave Moreau, a friend of both his and the Orientalist Eugène Fromentin. Berchère spent April and May of 1856 in the Sinai with Léon Belly, and from July to October, he visited Lower Egypt in the company of Belly, Jean-Léon Gérôme and the sculptor Frédéric-Auguste Bartholdi.

Four years later, he was chosen by Ferdinand de Lesseps to record the various stages of the cutting of the Suez Canal, which was finally going ahead after the first act of concession had been obtained in 1854 by Ferdinand de Lesseps from the viceroy of Egypt, Mohammed Said. Berchère's official commission to draw this colossal enterprise did not occupy all his time, and he undertook many solitary excursions devoted to contemplating and recording the surrounding countryside. It was, he wrote, "an exciting return to beloved, familiar lands, the enticing allure of something new, the elation of a traveller's existence, the sheer bliss of the unexpected." In 1863, Berchère published his memoirs in the form of letters addressed to Eugène Fromentin, to whom was dedicated the book, entitled *Le désert de Suez, cinq mois dans l'Isthme*. These letters, written simply and with talent, are a pleasure to read. The reader shares the author's enjoyment of absolute silence disturbed only by the passing of a caravan, and his fascination with the desert, "its unexpectedness, its grandiose poetry, its mirages and its shifting reflections... The desert insinuates itself into your affections, and you feel that, however stark and godforsaken it may appear, it is actually alive and throbbing with a life that is peculiar to it." He was understandably delighted to be able to return to Egypt in 1869 as a member of the official party for the opening of the canal, together with

Fromentin, Frère, Gérôme and Vacher de Tournemine.

Whether painting in Palestine, Syria or Egypt, Berchère did not make a point of depicting Islamic architecture or costumes. The classical ruins of Palmyra or an unusually large tree were of just as much interest to him. His oils and watercolours are those of a landscape painter in the widest sense, not of a convinced Orientalist who selects his subject matter to flatter the public's taste for exoticism. At times treated in a detailed manner, at others with large, loose brushstrokes, in browns, clear blues and greens, with occasional touches of turquoise, Berchère's pictures have great charm.

During the 1870s and 1880s, Berchère began to paint humble, everyday things: a jar of olives, pumpkins, fruit, loaves of bread. He kept these still lifes, in rich colours against dark backgrounds, for himself, not for public exhibition and sale. A founder member of the private museum in his native Etampes, he was on the committee from 1875. This museum now owns many of Berchère's watercolours, notably of the local countryside.

*Encampment*, oil on canvas, signed and dated 1869, 28 x 43 in (71 x 109 cm). Courtesy of the Mathaf Gallery, London.

# Maurice
## BOMPARD

Rodez 1857- 1936
*French School*

*M*aurice Bompard found exoticism in two places, southern Algeria and Venice. At an early age he went to Marseilles, where he studied painting before moving on to Paris. There, he became the pupil of Gustave Boulanger and Jules Lefebvre before exhibiting for the first time at the Artistes Français in 1878. A travel grant, won in 1882, allowed him to visit Germany, Italy, Tunis and Spain. However, his first Orientalist paintings, such as *Tunisian Butcher Shop* and *Harem in Granada*, were declared by critics to be too bituminous and reddish to be agreeable. Besides his portraits of members of socially-prominent figures, Bompard showed pictures of an imagined Orient, such as *The Favourite* and *Harem Scene* (Musée des Beaux-Arts, Marseilles), in which the sensual bodies of naked women gleam in the dark.

His picture *Butchers at Chetma*, shown at the 1890 Salon de la Société des Artistes Français, was a turning point in Bompard's conception of the Orient. During the 1890s and 1900s, he painted scenes of everyday life in Biskra and its neighbouring oasis, Chetma, with its beautiful gardens and eighteen thousand palm trees. Biskra, with crumbling walls and world-famous dates, and Old Biskra, a cluster of villages around an old Turkish fort, were no longer, by this time, the untouched spots enjoyed by earlier generations of Orientalist painters. They had become a favourite wintering place for Europeans, complete with hotels and casino, with a railway linking Biskra to Sétif.

Bompard was easily able to go from the high finish of academic painting to a freer, more modern technique, with pure colour applied in strokes. He excelled in subtle light effects. He took part in the 1900 Universal Exhibition in Paris and the 1906

Colonial Exhibition in Marseilles.
He was also a member of the Société
des Peintres Orientalistes Français
and showed his work at the Salon
des Artistes Algériens et
Orientalistes in Algiers.
He went on exhibiting at the Artistes
Français until his death, but these
pictures were mainly still lifes and
views of Venice. His paintings are
well represented in the Musée des
Beaux-Arts in Marseilles.

*The Sidi Mohammed Mosque, Chetma*,
oil on canvas, signed, inscribed and
dated Septembre 1890, 14.25 x 17.50 in
(36.8 x 44.5 cm). Courtesy of the Mathaf
Gallery, London.

# Gustave BOULANGER

**Paris 1824-Paris 1888**
*French School*

$O$f a ruined Creole family, orphaned at an early age, Boulanger was adopted by his uncle, A.M. Desbrosses, a civil servant in Santo Domingo. In 1841, Desbrosses enrolled him as a pupil of the history painter, Pierre-Jules Jollivet. Boulanger also followed Paul Delaroche's classes. There he met Jean-Louis Hamon, Henri Picou and Jean-Léon Gérôme, with whom he would develop the "neo-greek" movement. In 1845, he was sent to Algeria by his uncle and during his eight-month stay, made numerous studies of the people and landscapes, from Kabylia to the Aures.
The following year, he entered the Paris School of Fine Arts, winning the Premier Prix de Rome in 1849. During his stay at the Villa Medici, he decided in favour of two artistic tendancies: neo-classicism and Orientalism. A regular exhibitor at the Salon, he showed Algerian scenes such as *Arab Shepherds* (1859), *Kabyles Put to Flight* (1863), *Djeid and Sahia* (1865), *The Chaouaches of the Hakem* (1871) and *Taking up the Collection for the Feast of Aid-Srir, at Biskra,* works

treated with the precision of his friend Gérôme.
Professor at the Paris School of Fine Arts and at the Académie Julian, member of the Institut, he was a strong upholder of the traditional academic ideals.

*The Horseman*, oil on panel, signed and dated 1865, 22.75 x 32 in (57.5 x 81 cm). Courtesy of the Mathaf Gallery, London.

# Sir Frank
## BRANGWYN

### Bruges 1867-Ditchling 1956
*English School*

$S$ir Frank Brangwyn was a remarkable man who poured his energy and talent into every aspect of the fine and applied arts. The criticism and commentary during his early career was so voluble and flowery that it is difficult to gauge his real standing in his own time. One thing is certain, however: he was, and remains, an artist to whom one cannot be indifferent. He inspires either admiration or dislike. He received his early art training from his father, a poor Anglo-Welsh ecclesiastical architect who had gone to Belgium for economic reasons. As a young man, having settled in England, Brangwyn met the architect A.H. Mackmurdo and William Morris, the leader of the arts and crafts movement. He worked as an apprentice to Morris from 1882 to 1884, mainly occupied with decorative freehand drawing and with enlarging Morris's sketched designs for carpets, wallpapers, tapestries, etc. Throughout his life, he delighted in sound craftmanship and always considered himself a man of the people; heroic labour was one of his favourite themes.
Brangwyn's first journeys were made aboard cargo ships. In 1888, he visited the Dardanelles, Constantinople and the Black Sea, and the following year, Tunis, Smyrna and Trebizond. He made his

own way to Spain in 1891, in the company of Arthur Melville. The influence of the Scottish watercolourist broadened his sense of colour and loosened his technique. Brangwyn had built up a reputation for himself for fresh and forceful landscapes and pictures of life at sea, painted in near monochrome. But in 1893, the year he visited Morocco with the colourist Dudley Hardy, he exhibited *Buccaneers*, a vivid burst of paint which shocked the critics. Shown at the Salon de la Société Nationale des Beaux-Arts in Paris, this flamboyant picture was a great deal better appreciated by the continental audience.
This experience in exotic lands became a lasting inspiration for such works as *The Golden Horn, The Return of the Messengers of the Promised Land, The Rajah's Birthday* and *Market on the Beach in Morocco*, purchased by the Musée du Luxembourg. In these paintings, many of which represented fantastic, imagined scenes, Brangwyn showed a magnificent feeling for the pose and grouping of figures, with a theatrical exaggeration and a sense of drama. After 1900, his bold brush strokes and bright local colour virtually verged into the abstract. Soon, he practically stopped painting easel pictures and turned his attention to the applied arts : cartoons for stained glass windows by Louis Comfort Tiffany, carpets and a frieze for S. Bing's pavilion *L'Art Nouveau* at the 1900 Universal Exhibition, posters, designs for furniture and ceramics, etchings – each was of equal interest and equal importance.
Over the ensuing years, Brangwyn received many major commissions

for grandiose decorations, private, commercial, corporate and public. Many of these were in the United States, including the Rockefeller Center in New York. Although plans for a Brangwyn museum in Tokyo were frustrated by an earthquake, others opened in Orange, Bruges and Peking. Despite the outward extravagance of his work, Brangwyn was in fact an acutely shy man who spent his last years in Sussex virtually as a recluse. In 1952, however, he was given an exhibition at the Royal Academy, with nearly five hundred works, the first to be accorded by this institution to one of its members during his lifetime. Brangwyn was indeed the most internationally known and acclaimed British artist of his time, honoured by many foreign academies.

*"The Merchants"*, or *"On the Road to Samarkand"*, oil on canvas, signed with initials, 40 x 38 in (101.5 x 96.5 cm). Rodney Brangwyn collection, London.

37

# Fabius
# BREST

## Marseilles 1823 - Marseilles 1900
### *French School*

*Street Scene in Constantinople,* oil on
cardboard, signed, inscribed and dated
1871, 12.50 x 8.75 in (31.5 x 22.5 cm).
Courtesy of the Galerie Antinéa, Paris.

*E*ncouraged by Emile Loubon, his
professor in Marseilles, who had
journeyed to Palestine, Brest stayed
in Asia Minor for four years, from
1855. His paintings, with their
subdued colours and harmonious
compositions, conjuring up the
mysterious charm of the banks of the
Bosphorus, made his reputation. At
the Salon, he exhibited ceremonies
of the Sublime Porte, mosques,
houses of the Golden Horn and
Trebizond. He also painted a series
of pictures of *kief,* a word meaning
to have a sense of well-being, in
which groups of men are seen
relaxing in town or country cafés:
*Kief on the Road from Kerrassune to
Amassia (Asia Minor)* (1863), *Kief
in the Ok Meïdan in Constantinople*
(1867) and *Kief in Hamour, on the
Outskirts of Constantinople* (1875).
During the 1860s and 1870s, Brest
sent more classical vues of Venice
and the South of France to the Salon
Examples of his work are in the
museums of Beziers, Bayonne,
Nantes, Marseilles and Saintes.

*Kief, the Suyou Fonduk in the Valley of
Roses, Constantinople,* oil on canvas,
signed and dated 1861, 21.75 x 17.50 in
(55 x 44.5 cm). Private collection.

# Frederick Arthur
## BRIDGMAN

### Tuskegee 1847-Rouen 1928
*American School*

*T*he son of a Bostonian doctor, Frederick Arthur Bridgman was born in Tuskegee, in the southern state of Alabama. It was here that he saw slave markets before the Civil War, which left him a convinced anticolonialist. After studying at the National Academy of Design in New York, he worked for the American Banknote company. Dissatisfied with the turn his life was taking, he won a travel grant to Paris, where he studied under the direction of Jean-Léon Gérôme. He spent some time painting in the Breton village of Pont-Aven, where there was an American colony. During the 1870s and 1880s, Bridgman travelled several times to Egypt, to Algiers and to southern Algeria. He wrote a book, *Winters in Algiers*, published by Harper Brothers in New York in 1890, illustrated with his own paintings. He was an enthusiastic amateur photographer and worked from his own photographic prints, as well as his sketches made abroad. Besides scenes of Algerian life, such as *Moorish Villa at El Biar, On the Housetops, Algeria, Interior at Biskra* and *Bey of Constantine receiving Guests*, he painted historical reconstructions of ancient Egypt and Assyria, *A Royal Pastime in Ninevah, Pharaoh's Passage through the Red Sea* and *Funeral of a Mummy* In Paris, he had two studios on Boulevard Malesherbes, the fashionable area for academic artists, north of the Parc Monceau. One was decorated in the ancient Egyptian style, the other was filled with palm trees, textiles, moucharabies, Islamic tiles and narghiles, creating a Thousand and One Nights atmosphere, in which he adored dressing himself up in

Oriental costume. Bridgman, an amateur musician and sportsman, as well as a painter, led a brilliant social life. Married to a rich American, Florence Mott Baker, he did not have to sell his pictures in order to live, but he still went on painting every day. Although he was close to the academic painters, he admired Manet and Renoir, and his canvases, with their fresh colours, show a certain influence of the Chicago, New York and Paris, where he sold his work for fancy prices. After World War I, Bridgman went to live in Lyons-la-Forêt in Normandy, where he continued to paint Algerian scenes from memory, which became progressively more sugary and unreal. He spent his summers in Monte Carlo and Nice with his second wife, Marthe.

Impressionists. Bridgman exhibited regularly at the Paris Salons, the Artistes Français, the Peintres Orientalistes Français and the Société Coloniale des Artistes Français, as well as at the Royal Academy in London. He also participated in the Universal Exhibitions of 1878, 1889 and 1900. He rented private galleries in

*In the Courtyard, El Biar,* oil on canvas, signed, 32.75 x 46 in (83.2 x 116.8 cm). Private collection.

*On the Terrace,* oil on canvas, signed, 37.75 x 20.50 in (96 x 52 cm). Zeit Foto Co. Ltd. collection. Courtesy of the Galerie Nataf, Paris.

# Théodore CHASSERIAU

## El Limón (Santo Domingo) 1819-Paris 1856
### French School

*Jewish Women on the Balcony,* oil on panel, signed and dated 1849, 14 x 10 in (35.7 x 25.3 cm). Musée du Louvre, Paris.

*T*héodore Chassériau's Orientalist pictures combine the neoclassical idealization of Ingres and the emotive use of colour of Delacroix. Painted with sensibility and great intensity, they are amongst the most personal visions of the Eastern world. Chassériau's father, a government official who led an unstable and roaming life, brought his family to Paris from the West Indies in 1822. He left, alone, for South America, while Théodore's mother, the daughter of a French colonial landowner, returned home. The children were brought up by their elder brother, Frédéric. Théodore became a pupil of Ingres at an early age. Ingres had an enormous admiration for his talent, and invited him to Rome on his nomination as director of the French Academy, but Chassériau preferred to work on his own. He began his career with portraits and biblical and classical subjects, such as *Suzanne,* shown at the 1839 Salon and *Esther Dressing in Finery to meet Ahasuerus* (Musée du Louvre, Paris). These sensuous nudes, imbued with all the poetry of the Orient, show Chassériau's already developed taste for exoticism. At the time, a lot was written about this Creole's nostalgia for his native island, but it is more likely that this inclination was due to his adulation of Delacroix and his friendship with Prosper Marilhat, Théophile Gautier and Gérard de Nerval. In 1843, he finished a commissioned mural for the church of St. Merri in Paris, in which his scenes from the life of St. Mary the Egyptian were a blend of classical and Oriental antiquity.

Another commission, to paint the portrait of Ali ben Ahmed, caliph of Constantine, proved to be a turning point in his career. This picture was shown at the 1845 Salon, at the same time as Delacroix's very similar portrait of the Sultan of Morocco, Moulay Abder Rahman. Chassériau had become quite friendly with the caliph during his stay in Paris, when his unusual appearance caused a sensation in the streets and at the opera. This acquaintanceship led to an invitation from the Algerian

*Handkerchief Dance* or *Moorish Dancers*, oil on panel, signed, 12.50 x 15.75 in (32 x 40 cm). Musée du Louvre, Paris.

leader to visit his stronghold of Constantine. On his arrival in May 1846, Chassériau found that this astonishing town, perched on a sheer-walled crag, was filled with "invaluable treasures for an artist." "The country is lovely and brand-new," he wrote. "I am basking in the land of The Thousand and One Nights." He was fascinated by the varied ethnic types and saw "the Arab and Jewish races as they had been at the time of their earliest origins." He spent the rest of his two-month stay in Algiers. Although the city was too "Frenchified" for his taste, he was captivated by the light and beauty of the tones of the sky and sea. The landscape scarcely interested him as an artist, however; instead, he feverishly made sketches of people, in both pencil and watercolour. Like Delacroix, he found it was easier to enter Jewish than Muslim households, and it was amongst this community that he found most of his models.

His first major Algerian work was *The Sabbath in the Jewish Quarter of Constantine*, an enormous canvas that was destroyed by fire before any record could be made of it. The painting was refused at the 1847 Salon, but it was shown at the juryless Salon of 1848, where it was enthusiastically received by Théophile Gautier, one of Chassériau's most ardent admirers. He was not able to return to Algerian subjects until 1849, since he was obliged to finish the decoration for the Cour des Comptes, one of his many monumental religious and allegorical decorations for public buildings in Paris. By then, three years after his journey, his fading memories had become distilled into idealized images. Chassériau had made many studies of Arab horses in Algeria and these are the focal point of such lively pictures as *Arab Horsemen Carrying away their Dead* (Fogg Museum of Art, Cambridge, Massachusetts), *Arab Horsemen in Combat* (Smith College Museum of Art, Northampton, Massachusetts) and *Arab Chieftains challenging each other to Single Combat* (Musée du Louvre, Paris). Other pictures were solemn and melancholic scenes of domestic life, such as *Constantine Jewish Women on a Balcony* (Musée du Louvre, Paris), *Moorish Woman Suckling her Infant* and *Two Young Constantine Jewish Women Rocking a Child*. As for his sensual nudes, for which he posed Parisian models, *Moorish Woman Emerging from the Bath, Recumbent Odalisque, Oriental Finery* and *Interior of a Harem*, these evoked an Orient as imaginary and fantastic as the one he painted before his African journey. Chassériau had suffered from bouts of physical weakness since 1852, but when he died at the age of thirty-seven, the art world was stunned. Gustave Moreau began studies for a painting in tribute to him, entitled *The Young Man and Death*, now in the Fogg Art Museum, Harvard University, Cambridge, Massachusetts. Symbolising the fragility of success in the face of death, it was shown at the 1865 Salon. Many of Chassériau's paintings and sketches were donated to the Musée du Louvre by his great-nephew, the baron Arthur Chassériau.

*Ali ben Ahmed, Caliph of Constantine,
Followed by his Escort*, oil on canvas,
signed and dated 1845, 128 x 102.25 in
(325 x 260 cm). Musée National du
Château, Versailles.

# Alfred
## CHATAUD

**Marseilles 1833-Algiers 1908**
*French School*

$A$lfred Chataud was one of the first painters to settle in Algeria, and although he died virtually unknown, he sowed the seeds of the artistic movement which was to become the

*Orange-seller, Algiers Casbah,* oil on canvas, signed, 21.25 x 15.50 in (54 x 39.5 cm). Courtesy of the Galerie Antinéa, Paris.

School of Algiers in the 1920s. Chataud was the son of a banker, and his family intended him to work in an insurance company; he even spent a period in training at La Nationale in Paris. He soon gave up the security of this future career and returned to Marseilles in 1857 to take lessons from Emile Loubon, who taught generations of Provençal painters. Back in Paris, he studied with Charles Gleyre and frequently visited the artists Paul Guigou and Adolphe Monticelli, both from the South of France. In 1856, Chataud made his first journey to Algeria, where his family had property. From then on, he made short stays in Algiers and the region of Bône, spending his winters in Paris and returning to North Africa at the beginning of summer. He went as far as Tunisia and Morocco on some of these journeys. Although he painted landscapes around Mantes (where he lived for seven years), Fontainebleau and the outskirts of Paris, the paintings he sent to the Salons both in Paris and Marseilles were almost exclusively of Algerian subjects. Inspired by the melodramatic pictures of Henri Regnault (he made a copy in 1873 of Regnault's second-year painting submitted from the Academy of France in Rome, *Judith and Holophernes*), he painted scenes of a fantasy Orient, such as *Farniente* (Musée de Cirta, Constantine), *Sleeping Eunuch* and *Incident in a Seraglio* (Musée des Beaux-Arts, Marseilles), taken from Montesquieu's *Lettres Persanes.* He soon abandoned this style, but was still interested in groups of figures, such as *Negro Musicians in Algiers* (Musée des Beaux-Arts, Marseilles). In 1892, Chataud was called to

Algiers to settle a lawsuit over some property and decided to remain on a small family estate near Sidi Moussa. While he sent fewer and fewer paintings for exhibition in Paris, he was active in the creation in 1897 of the most important of the Algerian Salons, the Société des Artistes Algériens et Orientalistes, of which he became vice-président in 1904.

Chataud was particularly attracted to the old quarters of Algiers and Tlemcen, of which he made many small, often sketchy watercolours and drawings. These, such as *Mosque Interior, Sidi-Abderrahman Mosque in Algiers* and *A Nook in a Moorish House*, are simple studies of architecture and ornamentation, without any figures. Interested in Islamic art, Chataud made studies of jewellery, mosque lamps and Koran bindings.

It was Léonce Bénédite, the curator of the Musée du Luxembourg and founder of the Société des Peintres Orientalistes Français in Paris, who was behind Chataud's first one-man show in Algiers. On an official visit to inaugurate Algiers' municipal museum, he was surprised that Chataud's talent was so little known. An exhibition was organised in the museum by the artist Fritz Muller, but Chataud died a month before its opening. His work was shown posthumously at the Colonial Exhibition in Vincennes in 1931 and the Salon de l'Afrique Artistique Française in Paris in 1935, while Jean Alazard, the curator of the Musée National des Beaux-Arts of Algiers arranged another one-man show in the museum in 1937. Half of the one hundred and seventeen items in this last exhibition were lent by the greatest collector in Algiers, Frédéric Lung; others came from another art patron, Louis Meley. Since that time, Chataud's paintings had not seen until the 1982 exhibition in Marseilles, *Les Orientalistes Provençaux.*

*Fountain in the Algiers Casbah,* oil on panel, 24.50 x 12.50 in (62 x 32 cm). Private collection.

47

# Stanislas von CHLEBOWSKI

## Pohutynce 1835-Poznan 1884
### *Polish School*

*C*hlebowski studied in St. Petersburg, Munich, and then in Paris, under the direction of Jean-Léon Gérôme. After numerous journeys across Europe, he was attached to the court of Sultan Abdul Aziz at Constantinople for twelve years, from 1864. He painted episodes of Turkish history, such as *Sultan Ahmed III Hunting* and *Mohammed II Entering Stamboul* (Krakow museum), as well as scenes of everyday life. In 1866, he painted a moving portrait of the Algerian

*Musician in a Stamboul Street,* oil on panel, signed and dated 1872, 4 x 7.75 in (10 x 19.5 cm). Courtesy of Alain Lesieutre, Paris.

leader Abd el-Kader, then in exile (Musée Condé, Chantilly).
The artist then came to Paris, exhibiting *Tamerlane and Bajazet* at the Salon in 1878 and *A Circassian Second-hand Dealer in Constantinople* in 1879. In 1881, he returned to his home country and continued his artistic career in Krakow.

*Beggars at the Entrance of the Sultan Hassan Mosque in Cairo*, oil on canvas, signed and dated 1881, 29.25 x 21.75 in (74 x 55 cm). Courtesy of the Gallery Keops, Geneva.

# Georges CLAIRIN

### Paris 1843-Belle-Île-en-Mer 1919
*French School*

*Entering the Harem,* oil on canvas, signed,
32.25 x 25.50 in (81.9 x 65 cm). Walters
Art Gallery, Baltimore.

$A$ great traveller – he called himself a "vagabond by nature" – but the most Parisian of Parisians, Georges Clairin never achieved the greatness of his beloved friend Henri Regnault. Nevertheless, he was an interesting artist, one whose work merits a serious study.

Clairin studied with Regnault at the School of Fine Arts in Paris. With several other comrades, they went on their first journey together, to Brittany, which Clairin had already visited with his father, who had built the first Breton railways. He was to return many times. Clairin and Regnault joined up again in Spain, where they sided – briefly – with the republicans during the revolution. It was Clairin who posed in Madrid for Regnault's famous portrait of General Prim, sitting astride a barrel in lieu of a horse, and wearing the general's uniform. The two young men, penniless but always full of high spirits, went to Barcelona and Granada, where they haunted the Alhambra, "my divine mistress... fashioned of gold, silver and diamonds," as Regnault described it. It became their second studio. They made countless sketches of the Hispano-Moorish architecture, which they both used as backgrounds for paintings. Clairin joined Regnault in Tangiers, where the latter had arrived in December 1869. Morocco surpassed his wildest dreams: "The colour of the East, the odour of the East, its remoteness, its mystery, its prestige. Another life, another dream of life." They had barely settled into their Moorish house when the Franco-Prussian war broke out. Like many of their comrades, artists, architects, musicians, poets, they immediately enlisted, and fought

*The Palace Guard,* oil on canvas, signed,
31.50 x 26.50 in (80 x 67 cm). Private
collection.

side by side in the battle of Buzenval, in which Regnault was killed. Clairin stayed on in Paris until the end of the Commune, and then returned to Morocco, despite his grief and discouragement. He stayed for a year and a half. Mariano Fortuny visited him in Tangiers – Clairin organised an Arab fête in his honour – and they went on an excursion together to Tetuan. Clairin made another trip during this time, to Fez, with the French plenipotentiary, Charles-Joseph Tissot. Although Benjamin-Constant was part of Tissot's mission, it is not recorded whether he came with them. Fez, a holy city, was at that date not an easy place to visit, and Clairin was closely protected by some eight Moroccan guards. He found the journey frustratingly slow, for Tissot, an archeologist as well as a diplomat, insisted on looking for Roman remains. Clairin, coerced into digging, had little time to draw, but he was able to enjoy the continual fantasias given by their hosts, with four or five hundred horsemen galloping around them, firing off their guns.

On his return to Paris, Clairin was asked by Charles Garnier to assist with his Paris Opera House, the first of many decorations Clairin was to do for châteaux, hotels, theatres and casinos. After this long work, he set off again on his travels, to Italy, Spain, Algeria and Egypt. During this last trip, in 1895, he visited Upper Egypt with the archaeologist Morgan, and although he looked in vain for traces of Napoleon Bonaparte's expedition, he later painted several pictures of the general and his soldiers. He hired a Nile boat with his old friend the composer Camille Saint-Saëns, who dressed for the occasion in a Japanese robe and babouches, a fan in his hand. He then started across the Sinai desert with Morgan but, feverish, had to be taken back to Cairo where his life was saved, despite the fact that the city was cut off because of cholera.

Clairin, known as Jojotte to his many friends, spent his life between Paris and Brittany. An elegant, witty and agreeable man, his studio became a meeting point for theatrical, literary and artistic circles. He was a devoted admirer of Sarah Bernhardt and often stayed in the actress's Brittany home on Belle-Île.

Clairin's paintings were enormously varied in subject matter, including Venetian fêtes, opera dancers, flowers, landscapes and genre scenes inspired by his travels. He painted Sarah Bernhardt in many of her rôles and made a sensational portrait of her, now in the Petit Palais, which hung in her grandiose neo-Gothic house. His early Orientalist work was very close to that of Regnault, but with time, it became more and more fantastic and imagined. Scenes of war, such as *After the Battle, The Conscripts* and *The Carnage*, are frenzied and theatrical, while his women of the Ouled Naïl tribe, laden with jewellery and clothed in bright reds and oranges, are like members of an opera chorus. Prodigiously active, he showed his work at the Paris Salon de la Société des Artistes Français, the Salon des Peintres Orientalistes Français, the Société Coloniale des Artistes Français and the Algiers Salon des Artistes Algériens et Orientalistes. A multitude of oils, watercolours, pastels and drawings were auctioned

during his two studio sales and that of Sarah Bernhardt. Towards the end of his life, he published his memoirs, written by André Beaunier, *Souvenirs d'un peintre* (1906).

*An Ouled-Naïl,* watercolour and bodycolour, 12.50 x 10 in (32 x 25.5 cm). Private collection.

# Adrien
# DAUZATS

## Bordeaux 1804-Paris 1868
### *French School*

*The Convent of St. Catherine, Mount Sinai,*
oil on canvas, signed and dated 1845,
51.25 x 41 in (130 x 104 cm). Musée du
Louvre, Paris.

*A*drien Dauzats was among the first artists to paint the Orient with scrupulous exactitude and impartiality, but, although an initiator in this sense, his work never caught the public's imagination as did that of Alexandre-Gabriel Decamps. Brought up in the wings of a Bordeaux theatre where his father worked, he dreamed of being a scene-painter. Like his Scottish contemporary David Roberts, he drew from this experience a love of architectural perspective and dramatic backgrounds, which dominate small clusters of figures. In 1828, Dauzats began his long collaboration with the baron Taylor, a soldier, playwright, traveller, archaeologist and, at the end of his life, a philanthropist. After doing the first of many illustrations for Taylor's ambitious series of albums, *Voyages Pittoresques et Romantiques dans l'Ancienne France*, he accompanied the baron to the Near East on an official mission to obtain Mehemet (Mohammed) Ali's permission to transport the Luxor obelisk to France. These six months – from April to October 1830 – marked the awakening of his vocation as a painter. After a stay in the valley of the Nile and Cairo, came an excursion to the Sinai desert and the convent of St. Catherine, whose impressive site particularly enchanted Dauzats. In July, they set off again, this time to Jaffa, on a lightning tour of Palestine and Syria, visiting Jerusalem, Jericho, St. John of Acre, Damascus and the ruins of Palmyra and Baalbek. In 1839, Dauzats published his account of this journey, *Quinze jours au Sinaï,* which he co-authored with the novelist Alexandre Dumas père. In the same year appeared the baron Taylor's *La Syrie, l'Égypte, la Palestine et la Judée.* The hundreds of drawings Dauzats made from day to day, although done hastily and in difficult circumstances, are both precious architectural documents and full of human interest; he studied individual physiognomies, unlike many Orientalists who merely recorded costumes, arms and anecdotal details. It was from this source that he drew for years to come in order to paint his finished works.

A journey to Spain with the baron Taylor brought Dauzats to the notice of King Louis-Philippe and the royal family; he seemed to them an ideal choice as a chronicler to accompany the military expedition to Algeria, led by the duc d'Orléans, heir to the French throne. This expedition, in 1839, was both political and military, involving the pacification of the province of Constantine in preparation for a permanent French occupation. Dauzats followed the ducal tour from Oran to Algiers, to Bougie, Stora, Philippeville and Sétif. He was present at the submission of El Mokrany in Sétif and followed a division of three thousand men through the breach cutting across the wadi Biban in the Djurjura mountains, known as the Portes de Fer (Gates of Iron). Many of his drawings of the forbidding rock walls towering above the Pygmy-like soldiers at their foot were used in the famous *Journal de l'Expédition des Portes-de-Fer,* compiled by the poet Charles Nodier and distributed in 1844 to the officers who had taken part in the campaign. Dauzats's magnificent watercolours and oils of the defile,

of striking strength and austerity, are now in the Versailles and Chantilly museums.

From the time he first exhibited, at the 1831 Salon, Dauzats was greatly admired as a landscape and architectural painter. After 1840, however, he became increasingly involved in the onerous administration of the baron Taylor's philanthropical works (the

*Convent Church of St. Catherine, Mount Sinai,* oil on canvas, signed, inscribed and dated 1850, 25.50 x 19.25 in (65 x 49 cm). Musée et Galerie des Beaux-Arts, Bordeaux.

*Interior of Mourestan Mosque, Cairo,*
oil on canvas, signed, 28.75 x 22.50 in
(73 x 57 cm). Musée du Louvre, Paris.

Association des Artistes was founded
in 1844). Moreover, his multiple
professional obligations left him
little time for himself. In delicate
health, Dauzats's days of great
journeys were over. Haunted by the
memory of the countries he had
visited, he continued to paint
Orientalist scenes, but with a greater
number of details. These, although
still accurate, together with a certain
coldness of execution, make his
work of this time rather unreal,
lacking the freshness of the earlier
paintings. Dauzats died forgotten,
without having received official
honours, although as a man and an
artist, he had gained the respect of
his contemporaries such as Victor
Hugo, Prosper Mérimée, Théophile
Gautier and Eugène Delacroix. The
hundreds of sensitive drawings and
watercolours of his journeys, which
were Dauzats's most precious
possessions, were dispersed in lots at
his studio sale in 1869, and have
begun to reappear on the market
only during the last few years. His
oils are still rarely seen and his place
in the history of Orientalism, as an
exceptionally gifted and impartial
observer, has but recently been
acknowledged.

*Tomb of the Sultan Qalaun in the Maristan,
Cairo*, oil on panel, signed with monogram
and inscribed, 25.50 x 19 in (65 x 48 cm).
Private collection.

# Alexandre-Gabriel
## DECAMPS

### Paris 1803-Fontainebleau 1860
*French School*

*Turkish Children at a Fountain,* oil on canvas, dated 1846, 39.50 x 29 in (100 x 74 cm). Musée Condé, Chantilly.

Alexandre-Gabriel Decamps spent little over a year in the Near East. Although he never returned there during his long career, his paintings had an enormous impact, making him as famous in his day as Delacroix. Like many artists, he painted Oriental subjects before actually travelling to the East, imaginary towns and buildings as early as 1823, and Turkish figures in 1826 and 1827. The Orient was very much in the public eye because of the Greek war of independence, and when Decamps did travel, in early 1828, it was on a government mission to paint a picture commemorating the battle of Navarino, which had taken place in October 1827. He left for Greece without any great enthusiasm, accompanied by Ambroise-Louis Garneray, but the two artists found it impossible to collaborate. Decamps went on to Asia Minor, arriving in Smyrna in February 1828, where he set up an improvised studio. It was here that he painted his impressions of what he had observed during the day, without the customary help of pencil or watercolour sketches dashed off at the scene.

On his return to Paris en 1829, Decamps published an album of lithographs, but it was at the 1831 Salon, where he exhibited seven paintings, that he emerged into prominence. Many of his pictures are of Turkish soldiers, some are lively scenes of small children with curiously rounded heads, studying or at play, while others depict merchants and butchers in the gloom of their cramped boutiques. Still others are sombre landscapes or more ambitious biblical scenes. Early on, he developed the heavy impasto technique that was to be his hallmark, the brilliant light built up from the dark brown or black shadows in the manner of Decamp's glamourized, fanciful interpretation of the Orient, the thick, rich browns, ochres and blacks in violent contrast with the ivory and white light, however subjective and deformed, were for many years believed to represent the true Orient and so influenced generations of painters. Hailed as one of the leaders of the new Orientalist school after Delacroix, he was preferred by the bourgeoisie, who considered the

Rembrandt. Substance and technique, not the subject matter, came first. For this reason, Decamps has a real importance for the development of nineteenth-century painting, since it was through him that the texture of the paint itself was introduced to Diaz de la Peña and transmitted to Monticelli, Cézanne and Van Gogh.

*Turkish Cavalry Fording a Stream,* pencil heightened with bodycolour, signed and dated 1848, 26 x 38.50 in (66 x 98 cm). Musée Condé, Chantilly.

Romantics slightly suspect. His most enthusiastic supporters were the baron d'Ivry, the duc d'Orléans and his young brother, the duc d'Aumale (whose collection now forms the Musée Condé in Chantilly), and Richard, fourth Marquess of Hertford. This extremely rich English recluse, who owned houses in Bagatelle and Paris, spent his fortune on amassing an art collection, which he left to Sir Richard Wallace (now the Wallace Collection in London). Enormous prices were paid for Decamp's paintings, not only his famous Turkish scenes, but also those of game shooting, basset hounds and whimsical humanized monkeys. But having been brought up, at his father's express wishes, as a peasant, Decamps lacked the social graces and savoir-faire that were only too necessary at the time to obtain official commissions. He stood by while the commissions for the large historical paintings that he most wanted to do were given to fellow artists. Bitter and dissatisfied, he retired to the country, where he destroyed travel notebooks, sketches and studies. On his return to Paris from this self-imposed exile, he scored another eminent success at the 1855 Universal Exhibition, with sixty or so of his works devoted to different themes. Soon afterwards, his health failed, and he retired to the Fontainebleau forest, spending his last years repeating his own earlier compositions. Many of these late works were lost when his widow's house was destroyed during

the Siege of Paris in 1871. Decamp's watercolours can be ranked on an equal footing with his generally small-sized oils. Painted with great care, they are not preliminary studies for oils, but are finished pictures in themselves. His work is difficult to date, since his style did not change much, and different paintings often

bear the same titles. It was because
he was unable to renew his style that
even the critics who had been such
great admirers in the early days
eventually found his painting less
interesting. Even today, he has never
entirely regained the same level of
popularity as during his lifetime.

*The Punishment of the Hooks,* oil on
canvas, signed and dated 1837,
35.75 x 53.75 in (91 x 137 cm).
Wallace Collection, London.

# Alfred
## DEHODENCQ

**Paris 1822-Paris 1882**
*French School*

*A*lfred Dehodencq referred to himself as being the last of the Romantics. But despite his taste for movement, drama and violence, his preoccupation with individual physiognomies and his detailed reporting of each individual in crowd scenes classify him with the mid-century realists.

From an early age, he had a moody, passionate personality, and considered the Romantic writer Chateaubriand as his god. After studying with Léon Cogniet at the Paris School of Fine Arts, he began to exhibit religious and genre paintings. The revolution of 1848 and his horror at seeing victims lying dead in the streets inspired him to paint *The Night of 23 February.* These events, in which he was wounded, made him aware of the power of turbulent, angry crowds. Sent to convalesce in the Pyrenees, he went on to Madrid, where he was impressed by the work of Velásquez and, more importantly, Goya, who influenced his work. During this long stay in Spain, he painted a number of oils that showed Spanish life as heroic, sanguine, devout and fanatic.

In 1853, Dehodencq discovered Morocco – Tangiers, Tetuan, Mogador, Rabat, Salé. "It nearly drove me out of my senses !" he cried on first seeing this country with which he was to be so passionately involved. From 1854 until his return to France in 1863, he divided his time between Cadiz, with his Spanish wife and children, and Tangiers. During these nine years in North Africa, he made endless, brilliantly executed sketches, frenzied whorls that capture the movement of teeming life in Moroccan streets. He used individual studies of each detail to carefully build up his painted compositions. In many of these, exaggerated gestures and facial expressions, together with an often repeated trick of figures staring out at the spectator, give a caricatural aspect. Dehodencq's strident and brutal colours, with a heavy use of black, echo the violence of his subjects: *Execution of the Jewish Woman, The Pasha's Justice* (Musée Saliès, Bagnères-de-Bigorre), *The Thieves' Punishment, Arresting of a Jewish Man in Tangiers* and *Bastinado in the Casbah.*

*The Pacha's Departure*, oil on canvas,
signed, 46 x 35 in (117 x 89 cm).
Private collection.

Dehodencq, like Delacroix and Chassériau, was largely dependent on the Jewish population for his models, particularly in his interior scenes, such as *Jewish Concert at the home of the Moroccan Chieftain, Jewish Wedding* (Musée des Beaux-Arts, Algiers) and *Jewish Festival in Tangiers* (Musées de Poitiers). Although the paintings he had sent from Morocco for exhibition at the Paris Salon had been well received, Dehodencq did not know how to exploit this success. After his return to France, he found that his long absence had pushed him to the fringe of current art movements. He continued to paint Orientalist subjects, but even his moving picture of the last king of Granada, *Boabdil's Farewell* (Musée d'Orsay, Paris), was treated with indifference. He turned to more popular themes, sentimental paintings of children and narrative genre scenes but, in poverty and despair, he committed suicide.

Although Dehodencq had no great influence on his contemporaries, he was the first artist to pay more than a short visit to Morocco. Not only that, his drawings are amongst the most remarkable of the nineteenth century. The first people to rediscover and collect his work were Monsieur and Madame Alexandre Popoff, owners of a Paris gallery. Their collection was later sold in various auctions.

*The Moroccan Storyteller,* oil on canvas,
signed, 47.25 x 66 in (120 x 168 cm).
Private collection.

# Eugène
## DELACROIX

### Charenton-Saint-Maurice 1798-
### Paris 1863
#### *French School*

*E*ugène Delacroix's brief voyage to Morocco and Algiers has remained famous in the history of nineteenth-century art. Not only did it show French artists for the first time that North Africa held as much interest as the traditional pilgrimage to Italy, but it inspired some of the most exciting pictures ever painted. Delacroix's mother, Victoria, came from a family of famous

*Turk Seated on a Divan, Smoking,* oil on canvas, signed, 9.75 x 11.75 in (24.8 x 30 cm). Musée du Louvre, Paris.

cabinetmakers, Oeben and Riesener. Her husband, Charles Delacroix, had held various important governmental posts under the Republic, the Directory and the First Empire. It is now generally accepted, however, that Eugène Delacroix's natural father was that supreme diplomat and *éminence grise,* Charles-Maurice de Talleyrand. After the death of Charles and then of Victoria Delacroix, Eugène, impoverished, went to live with his sister, Madame de Verninac, whose husband had been an ambassador to Turkey. Trained, like Théodore Géricault, in the atelier of Pierre-Narcisse Guérin at the Paris School of Fine Arts, Delacroix was soon fully committed to the painting of *grandes machines.* Although a non-conformist, he was anxious to obtain government commissions and felt no compunction about working on those allegories and religious themes that were the staple of State patronage at the time. During the Bourbon restoration, Delacroix became interested in exotic subjects which he learned about through travel books, literature and accounts of topical events in the Near East, notably the Greeks' fight for independence. With his firm friend Richard Parkes Bonington (who taught him about the very English art of watercolour), he shared a passion for Lord Byron's writings; the poems of the eccentric and flamboyant Englishman, who died in 1824 during the defense of Missolonghi, were set in Greece and Turkey. Delacroix also talked with travellers, such as Jules-Robert Auguste, known as Monsieur Auguste. This wealthy painter and collector of Oriental art and curiosities had made his Paris house a centre for artists and writers newly interested in the Near East, as well as for Greek political refugees. It was Monsieur Auguste who lent Delacroix Oriental clothes and objects for his picture *Massacre at Chios* (Musée du Louvre, Paris), which caused consternation at the 1824 Salon. Described by Baudelaire as a terrifying hymn in honour of doom and irremediable suffering, it drew Delacroix willy-nilly into the Romantic movement, of which he

potentate reclining impassively amidst writhing bodies, produced an uproar. Other, less excessive Orientalist paintings followed, such as *Turk with Harness* (Musée du Louvre, Paris), *Mameluke on Horseback* and *Combat of the Giaour and the Pasha* (The Art Institute. Potter Palmer collection, Chicago).

Through his contacts in official circles, Delacroix was invited to travel with the entourage of the

became the reluctant but undisputed leader. At the 1827 Salon, he showed *Death of Sardanapalus* (Musée du Louvre, Paris), inspired by Byron's play. This violent and discordant picture, of an Assyrian

*Crossing of a Stream in Morocco*, oil on canvas, signed and dated 1858, 23.50 x 28.75 in (60 x 73 cm). Musée du Louvre, Paris.

comte de Mornay, special envoy to the Sultan of Morocco, Moulay Abder Rahman. The mission left Toulon for Tangiers, where it disembarked on the 25th January 1832. Delacroix was immediately struck by the dignified dress and bearing of the Moroccan people of all walks of life. They were, he felt, living figures from classical history. He noted: "Rome is no longer in Rome, the ancient world had nothing lovelier." The sizzling colours and

bright light deeply impressed him, too, and were to enhance his already masterly use of brilliant paint surfaces and vibrant harmonies of broken colour. Throughout his stay in Morocco, he made day-to-day pencil and watercolour sketches, annotated with a running text. These were contained in seven small notebooks, sold in his studio sale. These rapid, fluid sketches were to provide him with an inexhaustible supply of material for the following thirty years.

It was extremely difficult for artists at this time to draw Muslims, although Jacques Delaporte, the French vice-consul, invited some notables to the consulate to meet Delacroix. It was relatively easy, however, to persuade the Jewish population to pose. Amongst the many portraits Delacroix made was a charming one of the daughter of Abraham ben Chimol, a Jewish dragoman to the mission. One of the eighteen watercolours given by the artist to the comte de Mornay, it was auctioned in 1877 on the count's death. The mission set off from Tangiers to Meknès in March, accompanied by one hundred and twenty horsemen, thirty bearers and forty-two mules. Delacroix was able to sketch the sultan who, after the satisfactory conclusion to the negotiations, presented a lion, a tiger, an ostrich, two gazelles and four horses for King Louis-Philippe. After a short excursion to Spain while waiting for the official signature to the treaty, the mission finally left Tangiers in June and, after putting in at Oran, disembarked in Algiers on the 25th of the same month. During this three-day stay, Delacroix seems to have been able to

*Turbaned Black,* pastel, Musée du Louvre, Département des Arts Graphiques, Paris.

*Women of Algiers in their Quarters,* oil on canvas, signed and dated 1834, 70.75 x 90 in (180 x 229 cm). Musée du Louvre, Paris.

arrange a visit to the harem of the dey's reïs. From this, came one of the most famous of all Orientalist paintings, *Women of Algiers in their Quarters* (Musée du Louvre, Paris). Delacroix remained haunted by his African journey. Using his sketches and notes, he painted the scenes he had witnessed: religious fanatics, fantasias, a Moroccan caïd visiting a tribe, Jewish musicians from Mogador, the Sultan of Morocco surrounded by his guard. During the

imaginary, exotic and sumptuous Orient.

After Delacroix's death in 1863 (he had suffered from chronic laryngitis since 1842), his friends were entrusted with making an inventory of his studio. Pierre Andrieu (Delacroix's close collaborator and alter ego) catalogued the studies and unfinished paintings, while the critic Philippe Burty classified the some six thousand drawings. In 1929, the painter Maurice Denis founded the

1850s, Delacroix's Orientalist pictures became less and less realistic as his impressions faded. Painted with a Rubenesque exuberance, often of odalisques or of fierce combats, pêle-mêles of lions, horses and men, they conjured up an

Société des Amis d'Eugène Delacroix, which rented the artist's flat and studio in rue de Furstenberg in Paris.

# Ludwig
## DEUTSCH

**Vienna 1855-Paris 1935**
*Austrian School*

*The Scholars,* oil on panel, signed and
dated Paris 1901, 25.25 x 19.50 in
(64 x 49.5 cm). Courtesy of the Mathaf
Gallery, London.

*L*udwig Deutsch studied at the
Academy of Fine Arts in Vienna
before settling in Paris, where he
became a pupil of the history painter
Jean-Paul Laurens. He sent
illustrations to various publications
and painted historical and genre
subjects, which he exhibited at the
Salon de la Société des Artistes
Français from 1879. After 1883,
however, his pictures were almost
exclusively based on scenes from
everyday life in Cairo, such as *The
Caliph's Tomb* (1884), *Nubian
Dancers* (1886), *The Young
Favourite* (1888), *El Azhar, the Arab
University in Cairo* (1890), *Palace
Guard* (1896), *The Tribute* (1897)
and *Captain of the White Guard*
(1904). Little is known about his
visits to Egypt, but it seems that he
went there a number of times; works
dated 1886, 1890 and 1898 were
painted in Cairo. In rich, harmonious
colours, the architecture, clothes,
armour and arms are treated in
breathtakingly microscopic detail.

*The Healer,* oil on panel signed and dated
1891, 19.25 x 24 in (49 x 61 cm).
Private collection.

*At Prayer*, oil on panel, signed and dated
1923, 22 x 17.50 in (56 x 44.5 cm).
Courtesy of the Mathaf Gallery, London.

Besides this exceptional technical
ability, Deutsch had a nice eye for
small gestures and individual
expressions that give his people life
and character.

Deutsch's houses in the Pigalle area
of Paris and the South of France
were decorated in the Islamic
manner, with moucharabies, painted
ceramic tiles, textiles and metalwork,
probably used by him as studio
accessories, as was customary with
many academic artists of the late
nineteenth century.

He participated in the Austrian
section of the Paris Universal
Exhibition in 1900, winning a gold
medal. By 1919, his first name
appeared in the Salon catalogues as
Louis, not Ludwig, presumably after
his acquiring French citizenship.

He usually painted in oils on wood
panels, although some watercolours
are to be found. In 1909, however,
he painted an exceptionally large
canvas *Procession of the Mahmal in
Cairo*, applied with broad brush
strokes, quite unlike his earlier work.
He painted other pictures in this
impressionistic style at the same
time as his more elaborately detailed
ones, which he continued to exhibit
at the Artistes Français until 1925.
While his pictures are often
illustrated in the Salon catalogues up
until 1914, his work was curiously
enough almost totally ignored by the
critics of the time. It has, however,
become increasingly appreciated by
collectors over the last fifteen years
or so.

*El-Azhar – the Arab University in Cairo,*
oil on canvas, signed and dated Le Caire 1890,
64.50 x 90.50 in (164 x 230 cm). Private
collection.

# Frank
# DILLON

### London 1823-London 1909
*English School*

*"The House of the Mufti Sheik El Mahadi,
Cairo"*, oil on canvas, signed and inscribed
verso, 20 x 16 in (50.8 x 40.6 cm).
Courtesy of the Mathaf Gallery, London.

*D*illon's father was a silk
merchant who collected
watercolours; it was undoubtedly
through him that Frank showed early
on an interest in this technique.
Frank Dillon began his career
studying under the landscape painter
James Holland, a specialist in
Venetian scenes, and attending
classes at the Royal Academy. He
spent most of his life in London,
except for frequent travels, including
trips to Spain, Norway, Italy, Egypt
and Japan.

Dillon's earliest known visit to
Egypt was in 1854-55 and he
returned there several times: in 1861-
62, 1869-70 and in 1873-74. During
a later visit, he and some friends
took measures to restrict the
destruction of Islamic buildings in
Cairo, then in a ruinous state, and
made a series of watercolours, a
form of inventory, of certain old
Mamluk residences. He also opposed
the building of the first Aswan dam
which would result in the flooding of
Philae.

He exhibited a total of two hundred
and twenty-one paintings at the
Royal Academy and London
societies, such as the British
Institution, and took part in the 1862
and 1878 Universal Exhibitions.
The major part of his oils were
views of Egypt, such as *The
Colossal Pair, Thebes, The Sphinx at
Midnight, Nile Boatmen at Evening
Prayer* and *The Nile near the First
Cataract*.

*"Loggia of the Summer Reception Room (makad) in the House of Memluk Raduan Bey, Cairo"*, watercolour, 12 x 17.75 in (30.2 x 45.1 cm). The Victoria and Albert Museum, London.

# Etienne
# DINET

**Paris 1861-Paris 1929**
*French School*

*On the Terraces, a Feast Day in Bou-Saada,* watercolour, signed, 8.25 x 6.25 in (21 x 15.5 cm). Private collection.

*D*inet studied at the Académie Julian with Tony Robert-Fleury and William Bouguereau, although he soon rebelled against his professors' slick technique. His first pictures – he began to exhibit at the Salon in 1882 – were portraits and religious subjects. The course of his life was changed, however, when he was invited to visit the Algerian desert with a close friend, the painter Lucien Simon, and Simon's brother, an entomologist who was looking for a rare coleopter. This trip, in 1884, was the beginning of a life-long love affair with the country and its people.

His early Algerian paintings were above all investigations into vibrant luminosity, the reverberations of sunlight on the land being treated in an almost scientific manner. These small, figureless landscapes include *Rooftops at Laghouat* (Musée d'Orsay, Paris), *Msila Wadi after the Storm* (Musée des Beaux-Arts, Pau) and *Noontime in July, Bou-Saada*. By 1889, certain of his pictures, such as *The Snake Charmer* (Art Gallery of New South Wales, Sydney) and *Fighting for a Sou*, had begun to include human figures. People are depicted full-length and in the middle distance, unlike the close-ups in his later work, in which they are cut off at the bottom or sides in accordance with the technique introduced by the Impressionists. At this time, Dinet was still more interested in the matter of intense light than in the depiction of human emotions, which would be his forte later on. Not until 1904 did he make Bou-Saada his second home. Up to then, he had divided his time every summer between this locality, Biskra and Laghouat, doing studies of young girls dancing and laughing, of the richly apparelled and bejewelled women of the free-and-easy Ouled Naïl tribe, of shaven-headed boys playing pranks, and – something of major importance for Dinet, a deeply religious man – of the various stages of prayer. Although he spoke Arabic, which he had learned in Paris with his Orientalist friend Paul Leroy, Dinet was able to come closer to the Algerians through Sliman ben Ibrahim. The two men met in 1889, and became life-long friends. They

visited Egypt together in 1897 but found it disappointing. "Visitors to this country should view it from the standpoint of either tourists or scholars," Dinet wrote to Léonce Bénédite. According to the artist, nothing was comparable to the distinction and grace of the southern Algerians. With Sliman (and also with the Algerian miniaturist and illuminator Mohammed Racim), Dinet produced a series of books that were printed by the Parisian publisher Henri Piazza. These books,

*Young Girls of Bou-Saada Dancing,*
gouache on paper, signed, inscribed and dated 1922, 9.75 x 12.25 in (25 x 31 cm).
Private collection.

purchased on subscription by bibliophiles, included *Antar* (1898), *Le Printemps des cœurs* (1902), *Mirages* (1906), *Le Désert* (1911), *Khadra* (1926) and *La Vie de Mohammed* (1918). For *Tableaux de la Vie Arabe* (1908), a more ordinary edition, the black-and-white illustrations were taken from Dinet's oil paintings.

Dinet returned to Paris every winter to work up the pictures to be sent to the Salon or to the dealer Allard. After the founding of the Société Nationale des Beaux-Arts, in 1890, he left the Artistes Français, but was a regular exhibitor – and a leading member – of the Société des Peintres Orientalistes Français. He participated in the Colonial Exhibitions of 1906 and 1922, as well as taking an active part in the local Algiers Salons. The success of his pictures was enormous. Amongst the best known were *Abd el Gheram and Nour el Ain, Slave of Love and Light of my Eyes.* (Musée d'Orsay, Paris), *Sidna Yusef and Kotphir's Wife* and *The Courtesan.* Not all of them were scenes of play, love and prayer, however; he painted disturbing themes as well – mourning, illness, imprisonment, repudiation and conscription. Others were violent, such as the gory *Vengeance of Antar's Sons.* Dinet never painted replicas of his work "because his palette had changed," but his *Slave of Love* was often copied by other artists.

After World War I, Dinet's painting became looser in technique, with acid pinks, turquoises, mauves and blues. Dinet was by then little appreciated in France, as his style was considered too academic, although the French Algerians continued to hold him in high esteem. But Dinet's importance goes beyond any pictorial considerations. He became a Muslim in 1913; the sincerity of his conversion would help, he wrote, "in bringing about Franco-Muslim mutual understanding, a matter that is vital for Algeria's future." According to Ali Ali-Khodja, the nephew of Mohammed Racim, Dinet supported the claim for equal rights for

*The Springtime of the Heart,* oil on canvas, signed and dated 1904, 37.25 x 32.75 in (94.5 x 83.5 cm). Musée Saint Denis, Reims.

Algerians and sought to show through his paintings a philosophical and moral approach to Algerian civilisation and to the mysticism of Islam.

In 1929, Dinet, Sliman ben Ibrahim and Sliman's wife undertook a *hajj* to Mecca. The painter, who took the name of Hadj Nasr Ed Dine Dini, made no sketches or photographs, but depended on his memory to paint the illustrations for his book

at the Paris mosque before the burial in Bou-Saada, in his own mortuary koubba. The Musée National Nasr Eddine Dinet was inaugurated in the same town in 1993.

*Pèlerinage à la Maison Sacrée d'Allah* (1930). These were in grey camaïeu, not in colour, as he wanted to avoid any suspicion of having undertaken the pilgrimage for commercial purposes. At the end of the year, Dinet died before he could return to Algiers, where he had had a villa since 1924. A service was held

*Martyr to Love,* oil on canvas, signed, 28.75 x 38.25 in (73 x 97 cm).
Private collection.

# Rudolf
## ERNST

**Vienna 1854-Paris 1932**
*Austrian School*

*Man Seated on a Divan,* watercolour,
signed and inscribed Paris, 21.75 x 17.75 in
(55 x 45 cm). Courtesy of the Gallery
Keops, Geneva.

*R*udolf Ernst exhibited his paintings at the Salon de la Société des Artistes Français for nearly sixty years. But although they are now very much in vogue with collectors, they were scarcely mentioned by critics of the time. The Salon catalogues, however, often illustrated them, after 1900.

Ernst was the son of the architectural painter Leopold Ernst, a member of the Vienna Academy. Rudolf entered the Academy as a pupil in 1869, then left for Rome when he was twenty to continue his studies, having received a commission to paint the altar-piece for the Favoriten church in Vienna. He travelled to Spain, Morocco and Turkey. In 1876, he settled in Paris, eventually taking French nationality. His paintings were, until 1884, essentially portraits and genre scenes of pretty children and musketeers. From 1885, however, his compositions were almost entirely Orientalist, with Moroccan, Turkish or Hispano-Moorish backgrounds. His favourite themes were Nubian guards, mosque interiors, chess players, smokers of narghiles or chibouks, slave girls being caressed by their masters, harem women doing embroidery or being decked out in finery, and, occasionally, tiger hunts. Around 1900, he painted several pictures of Hindu temples, such as *The Sacred Pool* and *The Underground Temple*.

After a journey he made to Constantinople around 1890, he became interested in decorating faience tiles, a technique which he had learned with Léon Fargue, a Parisian ceramist and glass-maker. Ernst took part in the 1889 and 1900 Universal Exhibitions and then, around 1905, left Paris for Fontenay-aux-Roses, decorating his house with Islamic objects, which often appear in his pictures. He made replicas on a number of occasions, such as *Rose Picking* and *Interior of the Rostem Pasha Mosque, Constantinople,*

*Koranic School Pupils Taking a Meal,* oil on panel, signed, 17.75 x 21.50 in (45 x 55 cm). Courtesy of the Gallery Keops, Geneva.

probably on special request. He received commissions from official personalities in France, such as the maréchal Mac-Mahon and the duc de Castries, as well as in Turkey, where he painted a number of portraits during his journey.

The museum of Fine Arts in Nantes owns five of Ernst's paintings, given to the museum after having been shown on various dates in the annual exhibitions of the Société des Amis des Arts de Nantes. Other paintings are owned by North American museums.

*After Prayer*, oil on panel, signed, 20 x 24.75 in (51 x 63 cm). Courtesy of the Mathaf Gallery, London.

*The Favourite,* oil on panel, signed,
25.50 x 20.75 in (65 x 53 cm).
Courtesy of the Gallery Keops, Geneva.

# Arthur von FERRARIS

## Galkovitz 1856-Vienna
*Hungarian School*

*Reading the Koran,* oil on panel,
signed and dated Cairo 1889,
24.75 x 18.50 in (63 x 47 cm).
Courtesy of the Mathaf Gallery, London.

*P*upil in Vienna of the famous
portrait painter Jospeh Matthaus,
Arthur von Ferraris came to Paris to
study under the direction of Jean-
Léon Gérôme and Jules Lefebvre.
He had a considerable success as a
portrait painter in Paris, Budapest
and Vienna, where members of the
fashionable society sat for him. He
exhibited these portraits, as well as
Orientalist pictures, in the academic
tradition of Gérôme, with the Salon
des Artistes Français during the
1880s and 1890s. They included
*Narghile Smokers* (1887), *At the El
Azhar Mosque, Cairo* (1889), *Visit of
the Great Sheikh to the University of
Cairo* (1890), *A Descendant of the
Prophet* (1891) and *Bedouin at the
Arms Dealer'* (1893). He also took
part in the 1889 and 1900 Universal
Exhibitions in Paris, in the
Hungarian section. *MichMich, the
Performing Monkey*, shown at the
1892 Salon, was exhibited with great
success in Budapest the same year.
From 1894, the artist took part in
many annual exhibitions in Berlin,
and between 1904 and 1908, sent
works to Düsseldorf and Munich.

*Cairo Bazaar,* oil on panel, signed and
dated Paris 1890, 18.50 x 13.50 in
(47 x 34.3 cm). Courtesy of the Mathaf
Gallery, London.

# Eugène
# FLANDIN

## Naples 1803-Paris 1876
### *French School*

*The Conversation,* oil on panel,
12.50 x 5.75 in (32 x 14.5 cm).
Courtesy of the Galerie Arlette Gimaray,
Paris.

*E*ugène Flandin was born in Naples, where his father had been sent in an official capacity. The year after he made his debut at the Paris Salon with two views of Venice, he accompanied the French army during the 1837 campaign in Algeria. His *Capture of Constantine*, shown in 1839, was bought by King Louis-Philippe, but the canvas was torn by bullets during the 1848 revolution. Flandin's other Salon picture of 1839, *The French Army Entering Algiers, 5 July 1830,* is now in the Versailles museum.

In 1840, Flandin and the architect-painter Pascal Coste were sent on a mission to Persia by the Institut. At this time, the major Western powers were endeavouring to develop their political and economic links with Persia but, since 1809, France had had no official representative in Tehran. The mission, led by Édouard de Sercey, was supposed to obtain the maximum amount of information about the country's evolution under the reign of Mohammad Shah Qajar, and also to make a complete inventory of its monuments, both ancient and modern. De Sercey, unable to understand the subtleties of Persian politics, was soon recalled to France with his retinue, abandoning Flandin and Coste, who were fraught with misgivings about being alone in a country that was both dangerous and inhospitable once one left the cities. With two *saïs*, a French manservant, a disastrously bad Italian cook, horses and mules, they journeyed to Hamadan and Kirmanshah and then to uncharted areas in the southwest of the country, scarcely known to travellers. Later, they left the charms of Ispahan to cross the great arid plains to Shiraz and Persepolis. After two and a half years of hard work, they returned to France through Mosul, Aleppo and Constantinople. Flandin and Coste's impressive six-volume album on Persia was finally published in 1851, as was Flandin's more personal account of their journey. Two years later, at the 1853 Salon, Flandin exhibited an important oil, entitled *Ispahan, Entrance to the Great Mosque on Shah Abbas Square.*

He returned to the Middle East in 1844, this time going to Mesopotamia. The French archaeologist and diplomat Paul Botta was searching for the lost city of Nineveh, the ancient capital of the

miserable months doing drawings of these, which were published in 1850 in the album *Monument de Ninive.* However, by this time the English archaeologist Henry Layard had been able to prove that Kuyunjik, not Khorsabad, was in fact the site of Nineveh. Flandin continued to send oils to the Salon, such as *A View in Tripoli, Syria* (1857), now in the Lille museum, *Bazar Interior, Tehran* (1857) and *Sheikh El-Islam, the Damascus Chief Religious Dignitary, returning from Mecca.* He also published two more albums, *L'Orient* (1856), in four volumes, whose plates can sometimes be found in oils, and *Histoire des Chevaliers de Rhodes* (1864).

Assyrian Empire. He had abandoned the site of Kuyunjik for that of Khorsabad, where he had excavated some magnificent sculptures and bas-reliefs. Flandin spent six rather

*In the Vicinity of the Great Mosque, Constantinople,* watercolour, signed, 10.50 x 15.25 in (27 x 39 cm). Private collection.

# Mariano
# FORTUNY Y MARSAL

### Reus 1838-Rome 1874
*Spanish School*

*P*robably the most influential of the nineteenth-century artists who settled outside their home country, Mariano Fortuny y Marsal (often erroneously called Fortuny y Carbo) came from a family of artisans in Reus. Orphaned at an early age, he had to take on odd jobs to support his family. He was, however, able to take classes at the same time at the Barcelona Academy of Fine Arts, where he was taught by Claudio Lorenzale, a follower of Overbeck steeped in German classicism. In 1858, Fortuny went to Italy after winning the Prix de Rome. He made the first of his visits to Morocco in 1860, sent by the town of Barcelona to follow the Spanish military expedition under General Prim y Pratas, Count of Reus. Two years later, he returned to Morocco, commissioned by the Barcelona town council to paint a panorama commemorating the Spanish victory in Tetuan. Although he never completed this – epic painting did not suit his personality – he did, however, make many drawings and watercolours that he used as a basis for later paintings. In addition, the luminosity and intense colour of North Africa lightened his palette and eliminated the classicism of his early work.

It was during a stay in Paris in 1866 that Fortuny became friendly with the French academic painters, notably Jean-Léon Gérôme and Ernest Meissonier. He also signed a contract with the influential Parisian dealer Goupil. This agreement, giving Goupil exclusive rights to Fortuny's work, proved to be financially remunerative, but was later felt by the artist to be an impediment to his development. It was, however, thanks to an exhibition held by Goupil in 1870 that Fortuny had his first great success. The show was a sensation, not only for the Orientalist paintings, but also for his stylish recreations of the eighteenth-century rococo period and genre scenes, whose brilliant technique and strong colours had a great impact on young painters. Amongst his most fervent admirers was Henri Regnault... "He's the master of us all... Ah, Fortuny, I can't sleep because of you!"... and Georges Clairin, with whom the Catalan artist visited Tangiers and Tetuan in 1871.

Fortuny had such a convivial personality that he was always surrounded by followers and friends. In Paris, he had an entourage of his compatriots, while in Rome, he was so solicited by artists, travellers and collectors that he scarcely had time to work. An enthusiastic collector (a passion shared by his close friends Gustave Doré and Édouard de Beaumont), he filled his studio with arms, textiles, tapestries, carpets, bronzes and faiences. While his pictures were so sought after that he painted repetitions, his most important patron was William Hood Stewart, an American from

Universal Exhibition in Paris, the very fact of this patronage meant that Fortuny's work was not well-known to the European public. The news of Fortuny's death from fever at the age of thirty-six stunned artistic circles throughout Europe for he was widely acclaimed as an artist, and held in esteem and affection by his colleagues.

Philadelphia, whose Paris house was a haven for Spanish-speaking artists. Works from the 1898 posthumous Stewart sale in New York are now in American public collections, including *Arab Fantasia* and *Café of the Swallows* (Walters Art Gallery, Baltimore). Although Stewart's collection was borrowed for the 1878

*Arab Fantasia*, oil on canvas, signed and dated Roma 1867, 20.5 x 26.25 in (52 x 67 cm). Walters Art Gallery, Baltimore.

# Théodore
# FRERE

**Paris 1814-Paris 1888**
*French School*

*T* héodore Frère was one of the few French artists to paint Jerusalem, Beirut, Palmyra and Damascus, and it is sad that we have no account of his travels. Although he was well-known in his day, no monograph nor long articles have been written about him.

As a young man, Frère showed a strong talent for painting, despite his father's hope that he would follow a musical career. He studied under the landscape and figure painters Jules Coignet and Camille Roqueplan, then travelled around France, in Normandy, Alsace and Auvergne. He exhibited for the first time at the 1834 Paris Salon with a view of Strasbourg. A visit to Algeria changed the course of his life. He showed his first Orientalist work at the 1839 Salon and, from then on, painted only scenes of the Muslim world. Attracted by the sun, Frère travelled in Algeria for a year. During a second stay, he visited the fortified town of Constantine, which had just been seized by the French army.

In 1851, he went further afield, staying in Constantinople for

*On the Heights of Algiers*, oil on canvas, signed, 16 x 12.75 in (41 x 32.5 cm). Private collection.

*Encampement on the Outskirts of Jerusalem,*
oil, signed and inscribed Jerusalem.
Courtesy of the Mathaf Gallery, London.

eighteen months after calling at Malta, Greece and Smyrna on the way. He then continued on to Syria, Palestine, Egypt and Nubia, returning to Paris laden with material for future paintings and Oriental works of art, with which he filled his house. Frère, who received the title of bey from the Egyptian government, had a studio in Cairo.

Probably his last journey to Egypt was in the company of the Empress Eugénie, who was the main guest at the festivities for the inauguration of the Suez Canal in 1869. Thirteen amusing watercolours painted by Frère on this occasion are now on loan to the Musée de la Marine, Paris. One shows the royal party seated on the ground at an official

*Outside the City,* oil on panel, signed, 10 x 16 in (25.5 x 40.5 cm). Courtesy of the Mathaf Gallery, London.

banquet, liveried flunkies and Egyptian servants behind them, while another portrays the empress and her retinue on the backs of camels or donkeys, holding green-and blue-lined parasols over their heads. This last scene was also painted in oils by Frère, and shown by The Fine Art Society in the 1978 exhibition, *Eastern Encounters.* Other paintings by Frère are in museum collections in France and the United States (Chicago, Minneapolis and New York). Frère, who took part in the Paris Universal

92

Exhibitions of 1855, 1867 and 1878, continued to submit pictures to the Salon until 1887. Some, painted on canvas, were of considerable size, while many others were on small wood panels. Two, *Philae Island* and *Bedouin Encampment*, were owned by Princess Mathilde, a patroness of the arts and herself an artist. Théophile Gautier, himself widely

shimmering in a heat wave, camels picking their way over parched, cracked earth. Frère was not interested, however, in ethnic or individual facial studies; his people are never personalized. While his paintings give the impression of being detailed, their effect depends on a clever use of sharply delineated flat tints.

travelled, commented that the pictures' exactitude showed Frère's long familiarity with these countries of "gold, silver and azure." Other critics were more severe, reproaching him for his exaggerated colours. Certainly his popularity encouraged many minor artists to paint interminable pictures of an unreal Orient under impossibly blue skies. But Frère's contribution to the Orientalist movement was his talent for creating an atmosphere – the pale yellow light of dawn behind Bedouin tents, a glimpse of distant minarets

*A Market outside Cairo*, oil on canvas, signed, 14.50 x 24 in (37 x 61 cm). Courtesy of the Mathaf Gallery, London.

# Eugène
## FROMENTIN

**La Rochelle 1820-Saint-Maurice 1876**
*French School*

*Arabs Attacked by a Lion,* oil on canvas,
signed and numbered, 43 x 28.75 in
(109.5 x 73 cm). Private collection.

$W$hile the travel notes of this distinguished and cultivated man retained the original intensity of his experiences, his paintings ennobled, idealized and beautified the reality. "Processed by memory," he wrote, "truth becomes a poem, landscapes become pictures."

Eugène Fromentin came from a provincial bourgeois family of lawyers and judges. His father, Fromentin-Dupeux, a brilliant physician, was more concerned with his profession than with his two sons, while Eugène's mother was wrapped up in her pious devotions. This monotonous life in La Rochelle, an early unhappy love affair, and a lack of self-confidence due to his father's cold and authoritative bearing, made the young man withdrawn and dreamy. A brilliant student, he went to Paris in 1839. There, he took a law degree while continuing to interest himself in literature, poetry, history, nature and art. Finding the law office unbearable, Fromentin decided to take up painting seriously. Although he was at first influenced by his master, the landscape painter Nicolas-Louis Cabat, the artists he most admired were Delacroix, Decamps and Marilhat. They aroused his interest in the Eastern world, particularly Marilhat's showing at the 1844 Salon. Fromentin made his first visit to Algeria in 1846, only a quick journey from Algiers to Blidah, with its jasmin, roses, olive trees and orange groves. Astonished to find that it was quite unlike the Orient depicted by his predecessors, he soon realised that he could paint Algeria in a way that had never been attempted before. He returned in September 1847 for eight months,

this time going to Constantine and Biskra, on the edge of the Sahara. He paid a third visit in 1852 with his new wife, staying for nearly a year in Mustapha and Blidah, before journeying alone to the south, as far as Laghouat. This last sojourn was to remain in his memory forever. He brought back a mass of painted and drawn studies, many of which were auctioned in his studio sale. He found that the intense light of the verdant and cloudy Sahel, and even that of the parched and severe Sahara, was not blinding but made everything seem grey. As for the shade, it was transparent, limpid and coloured, not obscure and black, as it

*Arabs Hawking (Sahara),* oil on canvas, signed and dated 1865, 39 x 55.75 in (99 x 142 cm). Musée Condé, Chantilly.

*Egyptian Women in front of the Door
of a Dwelling*, oil on canvas, signed,
55 x 47.25 in (140 x 120 cm). Courtesy of
Christian Meissirel Fine Art, Paris.

was generally painted. In 1856, his important discoveries, together with his illustrated travel notes, were published in book form under the title *Un Été dans le Sahara,* followed, two years later, by *Une Année dans le Sahel*. These, together with his romantic novel, *Dominique,* and a classical work of art criticism, *Les Maîtres d'autrefois*, established his reputation as a literary man. Fromentin's pictures of tribal and nomadic life, particularly of horsemen in vast open spaces, began to change from around 1861. The subject were the same – aristocratic, pureblood horses, fantasias, groups of falcon- or gazelle-hunters. Strongly influenced by Camille Corot, however, he evolved new harmonies of subtle colours, which became nearly monochrome. He continued to paint and exhibit these Orientalist pictures, mostly from a sense of duty, as he had a family to raise. He felt himself condemned to paint perpetual variations on the same theme. In 1868, he made an attempt at grander, mythological subjects with centaurs, but this was a failure. In 1869, he was the officiel guest at the opening of the Suez Canal, when he took the opportunity of discussing with Narcisse Berchère the difficulty of rendering the beautiful scene, such as the setting sun on the pyramids. This Egyptian journey resulted in some of his best, although comparatively little-known pictures.

Although always dissatisfied with his work, Fromentin enjoyed great popularity with both American and French collectors. Such was the demand for his paintings that he often painted replicas; his most famous picture, *The Falcon Hunt*

(1873 Salon, Musée du Louvre, Paris) was, for instance, repeated in crayon, watercolour and oils. Although he never had a teaching atelier, he gave advice and encouragement to young artists, including Fernand Cormon, Henri Gervex, Ferdinand Humbert and Léon Lhermitte. Other painters, Adolf Schreyer, Georges Washington, Victor Huguet and, later, Henri Rousseau were to continue his tradition of equine groups in wide open spaces.

*The Encounter of Arab Chiefs,*
oil on panel, signed and dated '74,
25.25 x 32.25 in (64 x 82 cm). Courtesy of
Christian Meissirel Fine Art, Paris.

# Jean-Léon
# GEROME

## Vesoul 1824-Paris 1904
### *French School*

*The Sultan's Tomb,* oil on canvas, signed,
25.50 x 21.25 in (65 x 54 cm). Courtesy of
The Fine Art Society, London.

*T*he darling of the Orientalist
movement and lion of international
artistic circles, Jean-Léon Gérôme
was, during the second half of the
nineteenth century, one of the most
famous painters in the world.
The son of a prosperous goldsmith,
he studied Latin, Greek and history
at the local college of Vesoul in
eastern France. He enrolled at the
Paris School of Fine Arts in the
atelier of Paul Delaroche, from
whom he must have learned the love
for historical accuracy for which he
became famous. After the closing
down of the atelier following the
fatal outcome of a practical joke that
misfired, Gérôme spent a year in
Italy before returning to Paris to
continue his studies with Charles
Gleyre. He stayed for only three
months, but this was sufficiently
long for him to be marked by the
Swiss painter's teaching, although he
was always reluctant to acknowledge
this debt.
The success of his first Salon
painting in 1847, *The Cock Fight*
(Musée d'Orsay, Paris) encouraged
Gérôme and several fellow students
to paint other pictures in the same
vein. Hailed as *les Néo-Grecs* or *les
Pompéistes,* they presented antiquity
as witty, erotic and trivial, instead of
dry ancient history. While Gérôme's
comrades, Hamon, Boulanger, Picou
and Aubert, lived off this skittish
neo-Greek style for the rest of their
lives, Gérôme changed to a more
serious, remarkably realistic and less
obviously commercial approach. He
began his career as an ethnographical
painter with a small picture shown at
the 1855 Universal Exhibition
alongside his monumental,
neoclassical, *The Age of Augustus*
(Musée de Picardie, Amiens). He

had sketched the soldiers and guards for this work, *Camp Recreation, Remembrance of Moldavia*, during a trip to the Balkans in 1853. Realistically and objectively painted, its unexpected and unusual composition (always one of Gérôme's strong points) gave it its originality. In 1856, he visited Egypt. Four months were spent navigating on the Nile with friends, with four further months in Cairo in a house lent by Soliman Pasha. Over the next few years, he sent many

scenes of Egyptian life to the Salon, along with neo-Greek subjects, while gradually developing a speciality of seventeenth-century topics, recent historical events and contemporary genre scenes.

By the mid-1860s, Gérôme, by now a member of the Institut, was established and prosperous. He no longer needed the commissions that had been so helpful at the beginning of his career. Indeed, he found it a positive burden to finish the long task of painting his last official

*Leaving the Mosque,* oil on canvas, signed, 21.50 x 31 in (54.5 x 78.7 cm). Courtesy of The Fine Art Society, London.

work, the remarkably meticulous and complex picture *Audience of the Siamese Ambassadors at Fontainebleau* (Musée National du Château de Versailles).

He had in any case found a ready-made clientèle after his marriage to Marie Goupil, daughter of the influential picture dealer Adolphe Goupil. Not only did collectors – mainly American – slavishly follow Goupil's advice on buying contemporary academic artists, but Gérôme benefited enormously from

*Pelt Merchant of Cairo*, oil on canvas, signed, 24.25 x 19.75 in (61.5 x 50 cm). Courtesy of The Fine Art Society, London.

Goupil's worldwide distribution of photogravures and photographs of his work. In 1864, Gérôme was invited by the French government to be one of the teachers in the new ateliers opened at the Paris School of Fine Arts, which were to give this declining institution a new lease of life. He carried out this role for nearly forty years with zeal and conscientiousness and was certainly loyal and generous to his students. He enjoyed an excellent reputation as a teacher, and young artists – some two thousand – came from all over the world to study under him. Many were to become Orientalists: Albert Aublet, Eugène Girardet, Jean Lecomte du Nouÿ, Auguste-Émile Pinchart, Henri Rousseau, the Greek Théodore Ralli, the Turks Hamdy Bey and Khalil Bey, the Russian Vassili Veretschagin and the Americans Frederick Arthur Bridgman and Edwin Lord Weeks. He encouraged is pupils to travel, for stay-at-homes became, he felt, "slaves to formulas and routine." Gérôme himself loved exploring different countries and made many journeys, to Turkey, Egypt, Palestine, Greece, Spain, Algiers and Italy. He probably found travelling a great relief from the restraints of the Paris art world. Upon his return from a safari in 1868 (described by his travelling companion Paul Lenoir in *Le Fayoum, Sinaï et Petra* [1872]), this normally impeccable artist was practically unrecognizable with "his suntanned complexion, his long beard worthy of a Bedouin, his frayed garments, including a pair of Lenoir's trousers that had been shortened with only relative success." According to Gerald Ackerman, who has spent years researching on Gérôme, around two hundred and fifty out of six hundred or so finished works were of Orientalist subjects. Gérôme was mainly interested in contemporary Muslim Cairo and Constantinople. Certain themes occur again and again, with variations in the compositions, including guards on duty at a monumental door, Arnauts (Albanian soldiers in the Ottoman army) in their full white skirts; bashi bazouks (mercenaries notorious for pillage and brutality), naked women

consistent quality, are such that it seems impossible for one man to have painted so much; indeed, it is more than certain that he was assisted from time to time by collaborators.

The decline in Gérôme's popularity started during his own lifetime. As an opponent of the Impressionists – quite naturally so, since their subjective painting was diametrically opposed to his own careful, studied methods – he became involved in political skirmishes and was vilified

in slave markets or hammams, scenes of private and congregational prayer. On his return to Paris from a journey, Gérôme would quickly start working, with astonishing facility and dexterity. He used Parisian models, as well as props and costumes that filled his drawing-room, which was decorated in the Oriental style. The quantity and variety of Gérôme's pictures, of

*The Arab and his Steed,* oil on canvas, signed, 23.50 x 39 in (59.7 x 99 cm). Courtesy of The Fine Art Society, London.

as being old hat. When he died in 1904 he was, in the words of Gerald Ackerman, "buried with official praise, public indifference and critical acrimony." He had intented to leave part of his collections to his native city of Vesoul, but his gift was refused because of insufficient room. A victim of deeply-rooted prejudice, Gérôme became practically unknown in his own country. Not until 1981 was he given an official retrospective exhibition in France. By then, he had been reinstated as one of the most influential and imaginative painters of the nineteenth century.

*The Narghile Lighter,* oil on canvas, signed, 21.50 x 26 in (54.6 x 66 cm). Private collection.

*Arab and his Dogs,* oil on canvas, signed, 21.75 x 14.75 in (55 x 37.5 cm). Private collection.

# Albert Girard

**Paris 1839-Paris 1920**
*French School*

*P*upil at the Paris School of Fine Arts, he won the Premier Grand Prix de Rome in 1861 for his work *The Progress of Silenus.* During twenty years or so, he participated at the Salon with views of Normandy, the banks of the Loire and the Italian countryside, of which some can be seen in the museums of Mulhouse, La Roche-sur-Yon, Montauban and Montpellier. His Algerians paintings often show everyday life in Kabylia and Algiers, but also scenes such as *Sacrificing Chickens at Bab-el-Oued (Algiers Province)* (1875) and *Arab Hunters in the Blidah Mountains* (1883). Girard was also interested in the festivities in Algiers, when black dancers and musicians would perform.

*A Reception in Algiers,* oil on canvas,
signed, 20 x 28 in (51 x 71 cm).
Courtesy of the Mathaf Gallery, London.

# Eugène
# GIRARDET

## Paris 1853-Paris 1907
### *Franco-Swiss School*

*Bou-Saada Seen through an Open Door,*
oil on canvas, signed, 23.25 x 18 in
(59 x 45.5 cm). Private collection.

*The Prayer,* oil on canvas, signed,
21.25 x 15.75 in (54 x 40 cm).
Private collection.

*E*ugène Girardet came from a
Swiss Huguenot family, which had
boasted artistic members since the
eighteenth century. Eugène's uncles,
Karl and Édouard Girardet, were
painters who had travelled in Egypt;
his father, Paul, had engraved
episodes of the colonial war in
Algeria after paintings by Horace
Vernet, and his four brothers became
painters and engravers.

Girardet, something of a child
prodigy, was already able to sell his
drawings at the age of seventeen. He
studied with Jean-Léon Gérôme,
who encouraged him to visit the
Orient, although he already had
travel fever from listening to the
stories of his uncles' journeys. In
1874, he left for Morocco through
Spain. Then he travelled in Tunisia
and Algeria. This first contact with
the Muslim world enchanted him,
and from then on, he painted
Orientalist pictures. During the
1870s, he returned several times to
North Africa. Girardet was
particularly attracted to Algeria,
which he visited on many occasions,
not just to collect sufficient studies
and then return, but to savour the
landscape and to observe and
participate in the life. Some of these
stays were spent in Algiers and
Boghari, but above all in El Kantara
and Bou-Saada, where he met
Etienne Dinet, who later made the
oasis his second home.

Following the example of Gustave
Guillaumet, known as the Millet of
North Africa, Girardet painted
simple everyday scenes: herds of
goats gamboling in the dust, little
laden-down donkeys trotting along
between the red calcinated walls of
the gorges of El Kantara, and women
trampling their washing in the wadi

bordered with pink oleanders.
In 1898, Girardet visited Egypt and Palestine. In the Holy Land, he painted the tomb of Absalom amongst its fig trees and mimosa, and the impressive ceremony in the sanctuary of the Holy Sepulchre in Jerusalem. He painted two versions of this scene, *The Sacred Flame in the Holy Sepulchre*, with crowds of pilgrims tightly packed into the basilica lit up with orange and yellow flames. Girardet sent his work, which can be found in French and Swiss museums, for exhibition in Munich and Berlin, as well as the Paris Salons. He also participated in the Marseilles Colonial Exhibition in 1906.

# Gustave
# GUILLAUMET

## Paris 1840-Paris 1887
### French School

*Aïn Kerma, the Fig-tree Spring,*
*Tiaret Smala, Algeria,* oil on canvas,
signed and dated 1867, 55 x 75 in
(142 x 104 cm). Musée des Beaux-Arts,
Pau.

*G*ustave Guillaumet belonged to the generation of naturalist painters devoted to the problems of light and atmosphere. But more important, he was the turning point in nineteenth-century Orientalism. His descriptions, in writing and painting, of the primitive and austere life in the Algerian desert came at a moment when there was a great interest in France in the Algerian population, now that there were stronger politico-economic links between the two countries. Algeria was a French department like France's provinces, no longer a strange and exotic land.

Guillaumet had just won the second place in the Prix de Rome as a pupil at the Paris School of Fine Arts, when a chance invitation took him to Algeria in 1862. The visit started badly, for he caught malaria, from which he never entirely recovered, and had to spend three months in the military hospital in Biskra. But he was so captivated by the country that he returned nine more times.

During the 1860s, Guillaumet's Salon paintings tended to be melodramatic, such as *Evening Prayer in the Sahara* (Musée d'Orsay, Paris), *Razzia in Jebel Nador, Farming on the Moroccan Frontier* and the lugubrious *Famine.* His painting in the 1872 Salon, *Douar Women at the Moroccan Frontier,* which he repeated in oils, pastels and drawings, marked a new phase in his work. From then on, he showed the bleak, unchanging and impoverished existence of the desert people whose life he shared, whether under the black woollen tents or in the rough yellow clay houses of the little Saharan towns.

He travelled from Mascara and Oran to Kabylia, but preferred to escape the contaminations of European civilisation, going south to Bou-Saada, Biskra, El Kantara and Laghouat, one of the most advanced posts in the south. He made countless drawings and pastels of women drawing water from the wadis, horsemen, camels, sheep and wild dogs (he brought three back to his country house in France). For these open-air subjects, he developed a technique of tight, separate little touches of dry paint which defined

clothing in contrast to the sombre brown and ochre of the clay walls. Like Fromentin, Guillaumet was a literary man as well as a painter. His *Tableaux Algériens* (1888), a collection of articles that had been published in the *Nouvelle Revue* between 1879 and 1884, is an interesting record of the attitude of an European artist towards Algerian life.

mass and silhouettes. In the 1888 studio sale, four hundred and forty-nine oils, pastels and studies were sold; in 1897, one hundred and seventeen.

Towards the end of his short career, he painted women spinning or weaving in the interiors of their Saharan dwellings. The deep transparent shadows of the corners are strangely lit by rebounding sunbeams, the glowing red of the womens'

*An Arab Market in Algeria,* oil on canvas, signed with initials, 25 x 38 in (63.5 x 96.5 cm). Private collection.

# Carl
# HAAG

**Erlangen 1820-Oberwesel 1915**
*German School*

*The Street Musicians of Cairo*,
watercolour, signed, 20 x 14 in
(51 x 35.5 cm). Courtesy of the Mathaf
Gallery, London.

*C*arl Haag, Bavarian-born, introduced new and striking features into the technical development of English watercolour painting. With his deep, cheery, German-accented voice, he was a notable feature of every London private view.

He studied at the academies of Nuremberg and Munich, where he acquired a reputation for his miniatures. In 1846, he left Germany to see the world. After staying in Belgium, where he received many portrait commissions, he arrived in England the following year. The main reason for this visit was to investigate more closely into watercolour painting, a particularly English speciality that was as yet little practised on the Continent. After examining all the possibilities, he selected mineral colours for their quality of permanency, and evolved his own technique of applying pure colours in layers of wash, stippling with the point of a brush and then scratching out the colour to obtain highlights. It was during a convalescence, after his hand had been seriously damaged in a gun accident, that he formulated another original method, that of removing superfluous pigment, which had deliberately been laid on in extra strength, to arrive at the required tones. Such was Haag's ability that he soon became a member of the Old Watercolour Society, despite being a foreigner. However, it was his nationality as well as his competence that brought him to the notice of the German-born Prince Albert. He was commanded to attend Queen Victoria at her Scottish seat, Balmoral, where he painted two pictures for her.

In 1858, Haag made a trip to Cairo, Greece and Turkey, returning to Egypt that November. Here, he shared a house in the Coptic quarter of Cairo with Frederick Goodall, with whom he undertook many sketching expeditions in the desert. They entertained visiting artists and travellers, and gained quite a reputation for their hospitality. Jerusalem and the Holy Land were a must on any self-respecting traveller's list. Haag was no exception, and arrived there in time for the Easter festivals in 1859. At Queen Victoria's request, Sultan Abdul Medjid granted Haag a firman permitting him to paint the Dome of the Rock, often erroneously called the mosque of Omar. Jerusalem's Haram as Sherif, of great sanctity to Muslims with those of Mecca and Medina, had scarcely ever been painted before. He was also able to

*The Mosque of El-Ghoree, Cairo,* watercolour, signed, 19.50 x 13.50 in (49,5 x 34.3 cm). Courtesy of the Mathaf Gallery, London.

sketch a group of worshippers in the dimly-lit cave beneath the Holy Rock. This watercolour was later made into a print. Haag stayed in Jerusalem until June, before proceeding on to Samaria, Galilee, Damascus and Palmyra. He was able to study the life and character of the desert tribes and made a number of watercolours.

After spending a second winter in Cairo, Haag returned to England in 1860. He divided his time between his London house and his studio in Oberwesel, on the Rhine. After his marriage, he decorated the studio in his new north London home in the Egyptian style. By now renowned for his Orientalist paintings, which commanded exceptionally high

*"Amer, the Bedawee, Study of a Head under the Effect of Strong Sunlight",* watercolour and bodycolour, 14 x 10 in (35.8 x 25.7 cm). Courtesy of The Fine Art Society, London.

prices, he returned to Egypt in 1873 to collect fresh material. Here he was entertained by the khedive, through an introduction from the Prince of Wales. Over eighty of his works were exhibited in 1876 at the German Athenaeum in London, while his painting entitled *Danger in the Desert*, which had won a medal in Vienna in 1873, was shown at the Paris Universal Exhibition of 1878. Appointed as court painter to the Duke of Saxe-Coburg and Gotha, Haag won many awards and honours. His work can be seen in the museums of Blackburn, Bristol, Manchester, London (The Victoria and Albert Museum) and in the Windsor Castle collection.

*"Shipwreck in the Desert",* watercolour over pencil, 31.25 x 53.50 in (79.4 x 136 cm). Private collection.

# Victor
# HUGUET

## Le Lude 1835-Paris 1902
### *French School*

*V*ictor Huguet studied painting with Emile Loubon in Marseilles and then with Eugène Fromentin in Paris. While Fromentin never had a formal teaching atelier, he gathered a certain number of young artists around him, and Huguet's early work shows a certain influence of the older Orientalist's work in his choice of subject matter and cool palette. Huguet travelled to Egypt from 1852 on, and in 1853, he accompanied the marine painter J.B.H. Durand-Brager to the Crimea. Making his debut at the Marseilles and Paris Salons in 1859, he was a regular exhibitor at the Artistes Français with such paintings as *Bisharin Camp in the Libyan Desert* (1861), *Camp on the Walls of Constantine* (1865) and *In the Douars of Southern Algeria* (1877). He showed three pictures, one of which belonged to the art dealer Durand-Ruel, at the first Salon of the Société des Peintres Orientalistes Français, which was organised at the same time as an exhibition of Muslim art at the Palais de l'Industrie in Paris in 1893. He continued to send works to this annual Salon during the 1890s. Huguet's pictures were generally set

*Horsemen in front of a Mosque*, oil on canvas, signed, 18 x 15 in (46 x 38 cm). Courtesy of Alain Lesieutre, Paris.

in Algeria, Libya, Egypt, or, occasionally, Constantinople. He excelled in painting horses, and his pictures of encampments and falcon hunts, or of horsemen watering their mounts, crossing wadis or standing at entrances to great gateways were early on appreciated by collectors. Although his work is practically never dated, his technique over the years became more Impressionistic and his colours lighter and richer, with harmonies of ochres, pinks, reds and blues. Huguet's paintings are found in such museums as that of Nîmes: *A Slave Trader crossing the Suez Desert,* Rouen: *Ruins of a Roman Aquaduct near Cherchell,* Montpellier: *Arab Encampment in Africa,* Aix: *Algerian Horsemen* and Marseilles: *The Minaret* and *Caravan.*

*Market in Southern Algeria,* oil on canvas, signed, 26 x 38.75 in (66 x 98.5 cm). Courtesy of the Galerie Antinéa, Paris.

# Jan-Baptist
## HUYSMANS

**Antwerp 1826-Hove 1906**
*Belgian School*

*"Fathma",* oil on panel, signed,
8.50 x 6.25 in (33 x 16 cm).
Private collection.

*A* pupil of the Antwerp Academy
from 1843 to 1849, Jan-Baptist
Huysmans exhibited for the first time
in that city in 1850. After 1856, he
made a number of journeys to
Greece, Turkey, Syria, Palestine
(where he painted large religious
scenes for churches in Jerusalem),
Egypt and Algeria. He later wrote
several accounts of his experiences.
Many of Huysman's Orientalist
pictures were of simple, everyday,
scenes with strong colouring and
well-observed details of costume and
objects. In an unusual painting of
his, mothers bring their children to
be blessed by a holy man, the
sheikh, or master, of this particular
order of dervishes; this act was
considered to bring good luck.
From 1863 to 1891, he sent small
paintings for exhibition and sale with
the Glasgow Institute of Fine Arts
and at the Manchester City of Art
Gallery. He lived in Paris for nearly
thirty years, from the early 1860s,
and took part in the 1889 Universal
Exhibition. He then settled in the
Belgium town of Hove with his wife,
Maria-Catherina.

*A Passing Cloud,* oil on panel, signed,
25.50 x 21 in (64.7 x 53 cm).
Courtesy of the Galerie Antinéa, Paris.

# Augustus Osborne
## LAMPLOUGH

**Manchester 1877-
Bromborough 1930**

*English School*

$A$ugustus Lamplough, who studied
at the Chester School of Art, taught
in Leeds in 1898 and 1899. His early
work depicted cathedral interiors and
Venetian architectural scenes, but he
turned to Orientalist subjects after
visiting Algeria, Morocco and Egypt.
From about 1905, he almost
exclusively painted views of the
desert and the Nile, and market
scenes in Cairo. In common with
Robert Talbot Kelly and Walter
Tyndale, from whom he learned

*A Stiff Breeze on the Nile*, watercolour,
signed, 20.50 x 28.50 in (52 x 72.5 cm).
Courtesy of the Mathaf Gallery, London.

much, he was expert in applying washes of watercolour, which evoke swirling sandstorms or sky and water tinged by the dusk or dawn light. His ground colours were usually ochre or buff and cream. He used a curious backhand signature, although the latter occasionally occurs in a tighter form. His watercolours were used to illustrated the books he wrote, entitled *Cairo and its Environs, Winter in Egypt,* and *Egypt and How to See It,* the latter being a guide book for the Egyptian State railway. He also illustrated two of Pierre Loti's books, *La Mort de Philae* and *Egypte.*

Lamplough was particularly favoured by royalty. King Edward VII made a selection from Lamplough's pictures of Egypt and Nubia which the artist submitted to the sovereign at Buckingham Palace; other royal patrons included the Queen of Greece, Princess Beatrice, Queen Alexandra, the Khedive of Egypt and the Queen of Spain. Lamplough was a prolific artist, and frequent exhibitions of his paintings were held during his lifetime in London and the English provinces. In the United States, they have been on show in New York, Philadelphia and Buffalo.

*A Warlike Expedition in the Desert,*
watercolour, signed and dated 1913,
25 x 37.50 in (63.5 x 95.3 cm).
Courtesy of the Mathaf Gallery, London.

# Jules
## LAURENS

---

### Carpentras 1825-Saint-Didier 1901
*French School*

*Ashraf Palace Ruins, Manzanderan Province,*
*Persia,* oil on canvas, signed,
25.50 x 21.50 in (65 x 55 cm). Musée
Duplessis, Carpentras.

*J*ules Laurens, from an artistic
family, attended the School of Fine
Arts in Montpellier at an early age.
He worked for Baudouin, a scene-
painter in the local municipal theatre,
before going to Paris to study with
Paul Delaroche. He attempted,
unsuccessfully, to win the Prix de
Rome, but instead of starting his
career with the usual struggle for
official recognition, he had the good
luck to be invited to accompany
Xavier Hommaire de Hell on a
governmental mission to Turkey and
Persia. The French geographer had
already spent seven years in Western
Russia and the steppes of the
Caspian Sea. They left France in the
spring of 1846, going through Malta
and Smyrna to Constantinople,
where Laurens drew mosques,
fountains, costumes and portraits.
Various excursions were made to
Bulgaria, Moldavia and Brusa,
before they finally set off on their
arduous journey in July 1847; the
route to Persia, through Trebizond,
Erzeroum and Tabriz to Tehran,
had rarely been attempted by
Westerners. Twelve or fourteen
hours a day on horseback, often with
little or no food or drink, the menace
of cholera, terrible weariness,
miserable nights spent in
caravanserais with minimal comfort,
and practically impassable tracks
made their journey a nightmare.
Hommaire de Hell was temporarily
blinded from the sun's reflection on
the snow, while Laurens, delirious
with fever, was tied to his mule.
Unbelievably, he went on sketching
at each stop, filling sheet after sheet
with drawings of people and
landscapes.
Tehran, which they finally reached
in February 1848, seemed a paradise.

Mohammad Shah Qajar, who had been taught drawing as a young man by an English artist, Sir Robert Ker Porter, was not only most interested in seeing Laurens's work, but sat for his portrait. Laurens was soon in demand and did the portraits of one of the shah's aunts, Farah Khânoum, Persian notables and members of the European community, as well as drawing soldiers, camel drivers, street tradesmen, etc.

Sumptuous feasts and lavish hospitality were offered to the two painted, gilded and carpeted, the whole display surmounted by a proudly-floating tricoloured flag."

In the spring, Hommaire de Hell and Laurens left on an expedition to measure the level of the Caspian Sea, to verify the possibility of ancient communications with the Black Sea. The province of Manzanderan, with its rice fields, orange groves, cascades and luxurious vegetation, delighted them. In Ashraf, which they found enchanting, a handful of ruined

travellers. Laurens was particularly struck by the luxuriousness of the residence of the French minister, the comte Eugène de Sartigues, which boasted "some fifty servants, twenty-two horses, a calash, two Armenian women, one negress, one eunuch, ten falcons, an eagle, a pack of hounds, baths, seven courtyards planted with trees and flowers, an array of apartments and terraces, carved,

*Winter in Persia*, oil on canvas, signed, 44.75 x 74.25 in (114 x 189 cm). Hôtel de Ville, Bagnères-de-Bigorre (on loan to the Palais de Justice).

palaces were nearly swallowed up in a chaos of overgrown, mossy, humid greenery. The return through the plains of Khorassan and the great salt desert was desperately trying for Hommaire de Hell, still in poor health. After a stay in Tehran – where Laurens had the satisfaction of showing his large drawings to the shah, but was pestered by people clamouring for their portraits – the two men set off again, this time towards Ispahan. Hommaire de Hell, weak, and broiled by the fiery August sun, soon developed a strong fever and died in Djôlfa. After burying his companion, Laurens had a narrow escape from the pillaging hordes of tribesmen during the disturbances following the death of Mohammad Shah. He stayed for a few more months in Persia, but since foreigners' safety seemed uncertain under Nâsser al Din Shah's reign, he left Tehran in February 1849.

At the 1850 Paris Salon, Laurens exhibited the first of the many oils inspired by his extraordinary adventures, which had made him famous, partly because of his youth. He wrote and illustrated many articles about the Middle East in such magazines as *L'Illustration* and *Le Tour du Monde*, and made the plates for the magnificent album compiled from her husband's notes by Madame Hommaire de Hell. Laurens was invited to return to Persia by Prosper Bourée but instead, suggested such painters as Louis Tesson, Narcisse Berchère and Alberto Pasini, who was finally chosen. Although busy writing, engraving and painting, Laurens found time to create a literary and artistic circle around him, which included Prosper Mérimée and

Théophile Gautier, the engraver Félix Bracquemond, the Egyptologist Prisse d'Avennes and artists (many of whom had travelled to the East) such as Raffet, Dauzats, Vacher de Tournemine, Doré, Belly, the Princes Soltykoff and Gagarin, Pasini and Colonel Colombari. At the end of his life, Laurens wrote his memoirs,

which are full of invaluable information about his contemporaries. He left his watercolours and drawings to the School of Fine Arts in Paris and the museums of Carpentras and Avignon.

*Van Lake and Fortress, Armenia*, oil on canvas, signed, 33 x 49.25 in (84 x 125 cm). Courtesy of the Galerie Antinéa, Paris.

# Hippolyte
## LAZERGES

**Narbonne 1817-Algiers 1887**
*French School*

*Dreaming*, oil on canvas, signed and dated 1883, 28.75 x 26.75 in (72.8 x 68 cm). Musée d'Art et d'Histoire, Narbonne.

*L*azerges, who exhibited at the Salon de la Société des Artistes Français from 1841 to 1887, was a prolific painter of religious scenes which, as he himself admitted, were not easy to sell to collectors. Permanently in debt and pursued by his creditors, he found that the only way for him and his family to survive was to obtain purchases and commissions from the State. Indeed, many of his paintings are now in French museum collections, while his mural decorations are to be found in churches, chapels, cathedrals, the Orléans theatre and the Sorbonne. Lazerges first visited Algiers in the 1830s; he exhibited his *Courtesan, Remembrance of Algiers* in 1842. An auction of his work was held in Paris in 1858 and he probably settled in Algiers shortly after. His Orientalist paintings, often of full-length figures, include *Kabyles Harvesting in the Mitidja Plain* (1861, Musée de Perpignan); *Kabyle Caravan* (1876), *The Singer Fatma* (1877) and *Biskri, an Algiers Water Carrier* (1878, Musée National des Beaux-Arts, Algiers). Another auction of Lazerges's work in March 1876, consisted of wax paintings on panel, watercolours and drawings. He published a number of pamphlets on the Paris School of Fine Arts and the official exhibitions, composed music and wrote songs.

*The Dervish of the Mohamed Sherif Café,*
oil on panel, signed and dated Alger 1878,
28.50 x 22 in (72.5 x 56 cm). Private
collection.

# Edward LEAR

### Holloway 1812-San Remo 1888
*English School*

*"Constantinople from Eyup"*, oil on canvas, signed with initials and dated 1858, 15.25 x 9.75 in (39 x 25 cm). Courtesy of The Fine Art Society, London.

*G*enerations of English children were brought up on Edward Lear's Nonsense Rhymes, limericks and songs, but few knew the story of the extraordinary life of this many-sided genius, the most endearing of the nineteenth-century travellers.

Born the twentieth of twenty-one children of a London stockbroker who fell defaulter in the financial crash in the aftermath of the Napoleonic wars, Lear, in the break-up of the family home, was looked after by his much older sister, Ann. Ignored by his parents, subject to chronic epileptic attacks, and asthmatic, the child withdrew into emotional isolation. His decision to devote his career to landscape painting was taken early on. His already poor eyesight had been greatly strained by working on coloured plates of ornithological and zoological subjects, so further meticulously-detailed work became impossible. Not only that, his weak lungs could not stand the wretchedly damp and gloomy winters. Lear left England in 1837, and became a wanderer for the rest of his life. After living in Rome for several years, and having published three albums of Italian views, he began to explore countries off the beaten track, the Ionian islands and the Greek mainland, Turkey, Albania, Malta, Egypt, the Sinai desert, Palestine and, from 1872 to 1874, India and Ceylon.

Round, balding, bearded and bespectacled, Lear, at first alone, was later accompanied by his devoted Suliot manservant, Giorgio Kokali, who stayed with him for twenty-five years. Despite often extremely trying travelling conditions, Lear, hypersensitive to atmospheres, was wildly enthusiastic or gloomily overwhelmed by the new and absorbing sights and fascinating landscapes. Moaning, jubilating, suffering or rejoicing, he wrote down his feelings and impressions in his delightful and numerous diaries and voluminous correspondence. Lear was obliged to travel endlessly in search of new material for the drawings and paintings that were his livelihood. Although his Nonsense books brought him fame and some money, he incurred considerable expenses on his long trips. He sold his landscape albums, published between 1851 and 1870, on subscription, but lithography was a long and laborious activity. He thought, therefore, that by producing highly-finished oils, he would make his reputation as a painter. He laboured at these oils with patience and care, with help and encouragement from the Pre-Raphaelite painter Holman Hunt. They were, he felt, of far greater artistic worth than his sketches, although when commissions came for watercolours, he would be happy as well as busy for a while. The struggle to survive seemed never to come to an end for this lovable man of great gentleness, beneath whose unique humour lay such melancholy.

The first stirring of interest in Lear after his death began when Lady Strachey published two volumes of his letters in 1907 and 1911.

*"Jerusalem from the Mount of Olives. Sunrise"*, oil on canvas, signed with initials and dated 1859, signed, inscribed and dated verso, 15.75 x 23.75 in (40 x 60.3 cm). Courtesy of The Fine Art Society, London.

# Jean LECOMTE DU NOUŸ

## Paris 1842-Paris 1923
*French School*

*L*ecomte du Nouÿ is the epitome of academic Orientalism, with his highly finished, polished technique, his great attention to archaeological and architectural detail, and his themes taken from literary sources. He came from a noble Piedmontese family who had settled in France in the fourteenth century. His parents were collectors and his uncle, André du Nouÿ, was an official painter to King Murat of Naples. He studied with Charles Gleyre and Émile Signol before entering Jean-Léon Gérôme's atelier. Under Gérôme's influence, the young artist began to paint and exhibit pictures with neoclassical and Orientalist themes. Gérôme encouraged him to go to Egypt, around 1862, in the company of Félix Clément, who was commissioned by Prince Halim to decorate his palace of Shubrah, near Cairo. But Lecomte du Nouÿ only had eyes for the classical, not the Islamic, Egypt. His major painting, *Bearers of Bad Tidings*, exhibited at the 1872 Salon and purchased by the Musée du Luxembourg, was based on an episode in Théophile Gautier's *Le Roman de la Momie*. For this, he used documentation lent to him by the Egyptologist Prisse d'Avennes. By the time Lecomte du Nouÿ was thirty, he had enjoyed a considerable success. The State purchased other paintings, including *The Bird Tamer* (1870), *Death of Jocasta* (1872) and *Eros* (1874); he also received a commission to decorate a chapel in the Trinité Church. He won the second place in the Prix de Rome, travelled to Venice with the painter Charles Toché and then to Morocco – Tangiers and Tetuan – after the death of his new bride. As a result of this last journey, he painted *Jewish Woman in Tangiers* (1877), *Evening Prayer in Tangiers* (1879), *The Marabout Prophet Sidna Aïssa, Tangiers* (1883) and *The First Star, or the End of the Great Fast, Tangiers* (1894), exhibited at the 1895 Salon.

In 1877, he showed his outstanding *Doorway of the Seraglio: Souvenir of Cairo*, bought by Count Daupias of Lisbon. This picture's seeming photographic realism is but an illusion: in it, as was so often his habit, Lecomte du Nouÿ had put together an amalgam of details from documents. During the next few years, his main sources of inspiration were Victor Hugo and Gautier, for his large triptych, *Rameses in his Harem* (1885-86, shown in The Fine Arts Society's *Eastern Encounters* in 1978), *Oriental Women* (1884, Musée des Beaux-Arts, Caen), *Tahoser* (1887) and *Grieving Pharaoh* (1901). As for his famous *White Slave* (1888), the attitude of the languid, naked Circassian, is probably drawn from Gautier's *Émaux et Camées* or Gérard de Nerval's *Voyage en Orient*. Now in the Musée des Beaux-Arts in Nantes, she reminds one of Ingres' odalisques in *Turkish Bath*: indeed, it was said of Lecomte du Nouÿ that he was "Ingres painting in Gérôme's style." In 1895, the artist stopped in Bucharest on his way to

Constantinople, where his brother was architect to the Romanian court. Here, he painted portraits and frescoes in the Byzantine style for churches. He returned to Egypt to make studies for his *Grieving Pharaoh,* and later on visited Biskra, although he did not paint any Algerian scenes.

*A Sherif,* oil on canvas mounted on panel, signed, dedicated to Anaïs Beauvais, and dated 1878, 10 x 7.75 in (25.5 x 20 cm). Jordan National Museum of Fine Arts, Amman.

# John Frederick
# LEWIS

London 1805-
Walton-on-Thames 1876
*English School*

*"A Memlook Bey, Egypt"*, oil on canvas,
signed and dated 1868, 14 x 9.75 in
(35.4 x 24.9 cm). Private collection.

*J*ohn Frederick Lewis was perhaps
the most gifted on English artists to
paint in the East, with an almost
obsessive precision and wealth of
detail. His water- and bodycolour
entitled *The Hhareem* created a
sensation when it was exhibited in
London in 1850. But despite the
comment of the influential French
critic Théophile Gautier that it was a
combination of "Chinese patience
and Persian delicacy," his work was
little known outside his own country.
Lewis, a club-man and a dandy in
his youth, handsome and rather
aloof, was self-contained and
completely dedicated to his art.
Unlike many of his contemporary
artist-travellers, he did not write
enthusiastic and full accounts of his
journeys in diaries or letters. Even
the reason for his self-imposed
isolation from European civilisation
– he stayed in the Near East for
eleven years – has never fully been
explained. Lewis achieved
recognition as a distinguished
draughtsman and animal painter
before he was twenty. He came from
a family of artists and had received
training from his father, Frederick
Christian Lewis, Senior, a talented
engraver. He began to work almost
exclusively in watercolour from

about 1827. His first journey, to Spain and Tangiers, from 1832 to 1834, marked an important step in his career. It introduced him to Islamic architecture, changed his palette (he began to use washes of almost pure red, yellow and blue) and established his reputation. During the 1830s, he was nicknamed "Spanish" Lewis. In 1840, he sailed eastwards via Greece and Smyrna to Ezbekiyah quarter. He avoided the European community, saying that he enjoyed his life "because he was away from evening parties; he need not wear white kid gloves, or starched neck clothes, or read a newspaper." During his ten years in Cairo, he made countless sketches of the mosques, the shadowy covered souks and slender-pillared courtyards, the jostling bustling

Constantinople, where he drew numerous and impressive studies of mosques and the varied people found in the Ottoman Empire: Turks, Circassians, Armenians, Albanians. In the summer of 1841, he visited Brusa and later in the year, left for Egypt.

In Cairo, Lewis adopted Eastern clothes and lived as an Ottoman nobleman in a house in the

*"The Hhareem"*, pencil and watercolour, 18.50 x 26.50 in (47 x 67.3 cm). The Victoria and Albert Museum, London.

crowds in the narrow streets, and the interiors of harems, the sunlight filtering through the moucharabies onto the gorgeously rich clothes of the women. He also painted portraits: Mehemet (Mohammed) Ali Pasha, viceroy of Egypt, the young sulky-looking Prince Iskander, Madame Linant de Bellefonds, wife of the French engineer, and Sir John Gardiner Wilkinson, the noted Egyptologist.

Cairo in the 1840s was still a medieval town, before the establishment of the rail-link with Alexandria and the opening of the Suez canal brought a tide of European visitors. Even so, Lewis found Cairo too civilized, society chatter tedious and the occasional

"A Turkish School in the Vicinity of Cairo", oil on panel, signed and dated 1865, 26 x 46.50 in (66 x 118 cm). Private collection.

caller from England distracting. He liked nothing better than to ride in the desert "with solemn contemplation of the stars at night, as the camels were picketed, the fires and the pipes were lighted." In 1842, he made an expedition to the Sinai desert, St. Catherine's and Jebel Mousa. He also made several other trips outside Cairo, to Suez, Edfou, Thebes, and the cataracts at Aswan. Although he accurately recorded the temples, he made more of the groups of people and camels; his early training as an animal painter allowed him to be brilliant at these creatures, particularly hard to draw well.

When Lewis and his young wife, who was often his model, returned to England in 1851, they found that *The Hhareem*, his first exhibit with the Old Watercolour Society since 1841, had won rave reviews. His greatest champion, the writer and theorist John Ruskin, was terrified, however, that Lewis's jewel-like watercolours would fade, and urged him to turn to oils. Although Lewis followed this advice, he probably did so more from financial than artistic considerations. He was certainly one of the most accomplished known users of the difficult medium of watercolour, and although he taught painting, his pupils found his high standards impossible to emulate. Lewis resigned as president and a member of the Old Watercolour Society in 1858, but regularly exhibited his oils, always of Eastern subjects, at the Royal Academy; these paintings were often versions of earlier watercolour.

*"Interior of a Mosque, Afternoon Prayer"*, oil on panel, 12.25 x 8.25 in (31 x 21 cm). Courtesy of the Mathaf Gallery, London.

*"A View of the Street and Mosque of Ghooreyah, Cairo",* pencil, watercolour and bodycolour, signed and dated 1876, 23 x 17.50 in (58.4 x 44.2 cm). Courtesy of The Fine Art Society, London.

*"The Kibab Shop, Scutari, Asia Minor"*,
oil on panel, signed and dated 1858,
21 x 31 in (53.3 x 78.7 cm). Courtesy of
The Fine Art Society, London.

# Prosper
## MARILHAT

### Vertaizon 1811-Paris 1847
*French School*

*D*espite the brevity of his career, Prosper Marilhat emerges as one of the "classics" of the Orientalist movement. He was astonishingly active, accumulating sketches and studies, but due to his mental illness and premature death, he left hundreds of paintings only partially finished. While a vast quantity of articles was written about him during the nineteenth century, no single study had been made until Danièle Menu's 1972 university thesis. A banker's son, Marilhat spent his childhood in the château de Sauvagnat, in Auvergne. His father having settled in Thiers, he attempted, unsucessfully, a commercial career in cutlery, the local craft. Aged eighteen, he studied with Camille Roqueplan in Paris, and exhibited at the Salon for the first time in 1831, with a landscape of Auvergne.

Marilhat's opportunity to visit the Near East came when he was employed as a draughtsman to accompany a scientific expedition led by the baron von Hügel, a rich botanist, politican and soldier. They left for Greece and Egypt in April 1831. In the following months, Marilhat led a nomadic life, travelling through Syria, Lebanon and Palestine, returning to Egypt from Jaffa. His studies of majestic caravans and encampments in bleak deserts date from this period. Marilhat refused to accompany the baron, who was setting off for India, for he had become passionately attracted to Egypt. Not only did he see faces which he found exactly resembled those of ancient Egyptian sculptures, but he was particularly struck by the nobility and grandeur of the land and its people. Late 1832 found him in Alexandria where he was "painting portraits in order to live and doing studies in order to learn." He painted Mehemet (Mohammed) Ali and the Egyptologist Prisse d'Avennes, as well as local notables, and even designed stage sets for the local theatre. The fees from these activities allowed him to prolong his stay, and he explored the Nile delta until May of the following year, when he returned aboard the Sphinx, which was carrying the Luxor obelisk.

Marilhat's works in the 1834 Salon were a revelation to the public. The critics, particularly Théophile Gautier, were unanimously favourable. The famous painting of *Ezbekiyah Square and the Copt Quarter in Cairo* inspired Gautier with "a nostalgia for the Eastern world, in which I had never set foot. It seemed to me that I had just experienced the revelation of my true fatherland, and when my gaze detached itself from this ardent painting, I felt as if I had been exiled." Marilhat continued to paint portraits and European landscapes, as well as Orientalist subjects. But he began displaying signs of mental disturbance early on. Although his eight paintings at the 1844 Salon were a triumph, elevating him to the height of his reputation, he felt that he deserved greater attention. The progress of his illness prevented him from carrying out his plans to return to Egypt and he was instead given an annual pension by the French government, thanks to the initiative of Prosper Mérimée and the painter Camille Corot. It was too late; Marilhat died, mad, in Paris after a short stay in his family's town, Thiers.

various artists, many of which are now in the Cabinet des Estampes in Paris and the British Museum, London. This success meant, however, that many copies of his paintings were made both during his lifetime and in the years following his death. His oils, rarely seen on the market, are to be found in many museum collections in Europe and the United States.

Marilhat's delicate drawings, often heightened with touches of sanguine and chalk, show his concern for accuracy. But his oil paintings, despite his sincerity and true appreciation of the East, were less objective: his landscapes, in over-rich colours, bathed in perpetual sunlight, without nuances of half-tones, are not always to the modern taste. His work was particularly well-known in his lifetime through the publications of engravings by

*Ruins of the al-Hakim Mosque, Cairo,* oil on canvas, signed, 33.25 x 51.25 in (84.5 x 130.5 cm). Musée du Louvre, Paris.

# Arthur
## MELVILLE

### East Linton 1855-Witley 1904
*Scottish School*

*"The Turkish Bazaar, Cairo",*
watercolour and bodycolour,
signed and dated Cairo 1881,
21.50 x 14.75 in (54.5 x 37.1 cm).
Courtesy of The Fine Art Society, London.

**A**rthur Melville was interested in light and colour to the exclusion of anecdotal detail, and was one of the most unusual and personal watercolour artists of his time. He was an influential member of the group of progressive artists in Glasgow, formed around 1880 to 1895, known at the time as the "Glasgow Boys." They nearly all supplemented their training abroad, in Brussels, Munich, Düsseldorf and Paris. French academic training was then one of the best and most thorough in Europe, and so Melville came to Paris in 1878 to study at the Académie Julian.

In the autumn of 1880, he went to Egypt. He soon became a popular member of the English colony, and sent back his work to art dealers at home. From then on, he worked almost exclusively in watercolours. He developed a technique of placing his colour on wet paper impregnated with Chinese white. This was done without the customary support of a preparatory drawing. The small, concentrated patches of colour, plum, russet and blue, with occasional touches of green and yellow, contrasted with the large areas of plain wash.

In March 1882, Melville sailed with Sir Arthur Stepney on a boat down the Red Sea to Jidda, and then from Aden across to India, as far as Karachi. He left India almost immediately for Muscat, where he found that "the Arabs with their pistols, spears and swords, dark skins and supple drapery were a feast for the gods. Nothing could be more striking." It was at first planned that he and Sir Arthur should go on horseback through Persia. In the end, the project was abandoned and Melville rode across Asia Minor from Bagdad to the Black Sea. He had already painted a "cartload" of watercolours, for he found he could do five, or sometimes as many as eight a week, and these he sent home, away from danger. Often riding at night, taking catnaps whenever possible, he was once pursued by a group of over a hundred outlaws, with gunshots whistling around his head. He continued his journey to Mosul and Diarbeker, having suffered terribly from fever. Again attacked by robbers, he was left for dead, naked in the desert. He managed to drag himself to a nearby village and later joined the punitive expedition against these tribesmen, when he was able to recover his effects, which included his Scottish plaid and Bible. Detained by the local pasha, who was inclined to consider his European guest as a British spy, Melville was finally allowed to continue his journey to Constantinople. On his return to Edinburgh, his friends dismissed his stories of his adventures as travellers' tales. His name, however, was forever to be associated with his journey. Considered as dangerously avant-garde by the Royal Scottish Academy, Melville showed his work at the Royal Watercolour Society in London. In 1893, he and the "Glasgow Boys" held an exhibition at the London Grafton Gallery with James Whistler and the French artists Edgar Degas and Jean-François Raffaëlli. The impressionistic work of the Scots, sent to the St. Louis

exhibition, caused a sensation. Melville made further journeys, to Algeria, Morocco and Spain, which he visited in 1891 with the painter Frank Brangwyn. He went to Venice for the first time in 1894, but found it tame and conventional after the East. It was during one of his trips to Spain that he contracted typhoid, from which he died.

*An Islamic Courtyard,* watercolour, 20.75 x 15 in (53 x 38 cm). Private collection.

# Leopold Carl
# MÜLLER

## Dresden 1834-Vienna 1892
### *Austrian School*

*L*eopold Carl Müller was an outstanding painter, who had a strong influence on the Viennese school of Orientalists.

After studying with his father, the lithographer Leopold Müller, he became the pupil of Karl von Blaas and Christian Ruben at the Vienna Academy of Fine Arts. At first, he painted historical subjects, portraits and Italian landscapes, while contributing to a Viennese satirical magazine, *Figaro*. He made the first of his nine visits to Cairo in the winter of 1873-74; he not only enjoyed travelling, but felt that the climate would be good for his health, since he feared that he had inherited the family tendency to weak lungs. He launched into a method of working, new to him, that of making studies from nature, which he worked up into finished paintings on his return home. After this first trip, he hurried back to Vienna through Constantinople instead of visiting Syria, as he had planned, since he did not want his impressions falsified by having to wait too long to set them down on canvas. He brought back some fifteen Oriental costumes, which he later used as accessories in his pictures. That winter, he finished his large painting

entitled *Bedouin Camped Near the Pyramids* which was exhibited at the Kunstlerhaus and bought by the Belvedere (Osterreichische Galerie). The following year, in February 1875, he was back in Cairo, where he invited the Viennese artist Hans Makart to join him in the winter of 1875-76. Makart, whose Orient was purely imaginary, did not share Müller's enthusiasm for painting in the sun. Amongst the other painters who joined them was the fashionable portrait painter Franz von Lenbach. Müller, often in financial difficulties, began to receive commissions, including one for his *Marketplace outside Cairo*. This painting, finished in 1878, is considered one of his most important works, although Müller, often dissatisfied with his own efforts, did not like it. It was frequently copied, although Müller used to tell his pupils to choose something better. In 1877, he finished his *Palm Frond Vendor*, typical of the striking single-figure studies at which Müller excelled. He also accepted a teaching position at the Academy of Fine Arts, but was given permission to visit Cairo again before reluctantly taking up his duties. During this time, in the winter of 1877-78, he made further drawings for Georg Ebers, the German Egyptologist and novelist, who wrote about Egyptian life in the pharaonic times. He considered one of his most successful trips the one he made in 1881 to Upper Egypt, staying for nearly two months in Aswan, by which he was enormously impressed.

Although Müller found a ready market for his paintings due to the English visitors wintering in Cairo, finished works were *The Tumbler*, similar to the painting of his pupil Franz Kosler, and *Sugar Cane Market*, which reveal his genius for original crowd compositions, with elegant colouring and remarkably modelled figures and faces. A year after Müller's death, his portrait *Nefusa,* now in the Osterreichische Galerie, Vienna, which owns a number of his works, was purchased by Emperor Franz Joseph of Austria.

*Marketplace outside Cairo*, oil on canvas, signed and dated 1878, 53.50 x 85 in (136 x 216 cm). Österreichische Galerie, Vienna.

he had been advised by the Prince of Wales in 1875 to send his work to London. His paintings had therefore been appreciated there for a number of years, and in 1882, he paid a visit to the English capital. Amongst the oils owned by English collectors were *The Drinking Fountain, The Backgammon Players* and *Interior of an Arab Dwelling.*
Müller continued to visit Egypt until 1886. Amongst the last of his

# Alberto
# PASINI

## Busseto 1826-Cavoretto 1899
### *Italian School*

*The Arrival of the Pasha*, oil on canvas,
signed, 20.75 x 14 in (52.7 x 35.5 cm).
Private collection.

Alberto Pasini's technical skill,
sense of colour harmony and
excellent treatment of light make one
regret that his delightful paintings
are so rarely to be found.
Born in the duchy of Parma, he
became an orphan at an early age.
After studying lithography at the
Academy of Fine Arts in Parma, he
published and illustrated an album
on the architecture and history of the
region. This was, however,
insufficient for him to live on. He
left Italy for Paris in 1851. It was
thanks to Théodore Chassériau that
Pasini met the diplomat Prosper
Bourée, who was about to leave on
an official mission to counteract the
Russian influence in Nâsser-al Din
Shah's Persia at the time of the
Crimean war. Pasini was invited to
accompany Bourée as his personal
painter, together with the author, the
comte Arthur de Gobineau. The
latter, at first hostile towards Pasini,
omitted to mention the artist's name
in his book entitled *Trois ans en Asie
1855-58.*
In March 1855, Pasini set off
through Egypt, Saudi Arabia, South
Yemen and the Persian Gulf, finally
arriving in Teheran, where he spent a
year and a half. Not only were many
of his trips around Persia made in
the company of the shah, but the
sovereign commissioned a number
of paintings. Pasini returned in 1856,
this time via the Black Sea and
Constantinople. Once back in Paris,
he began to send views of Persia,
Arabia, Azerbaijan and Syria to the
annual Salons. He was able to meet
up with old Persian hands in Jules
Laurens's studio, such as the artists

*The Prisonners,* oil on canvas, signed
and dated 1880, 16.75 x 13.25 in
(42.5 x 33.5 cm). Private collection.

Prince Alexis Soltykoff, Eugène Flandin and Colonel F. Colombari. His high expectations fulfilled after his adventure, Pasini continued to travel: Constantinople in 1868-69, Asia Minor, Syria and Lebanon in 1873, frequent visits to Venice, and two journeys to Spain, one in the company of Jean-Léon Gérôme and Albert Aublet. After dividing the rest of his time between Paris and his villa in Cavoretto, near Turin, he finally settled down in Italy to concentrated on agriculture as well as painting.

Pasini was probably the best-known Orientalist artist of foreign origin in France. He found a ready sale for his canvases through the Parisian dealer Goupil and had a faithful following of American visitors to the Salon; many examples of his work are now to be found in American and Canadian museums. He sent paintings on show to Florence and, more particularly, to his city of adoption, Turin. At the national exhibition in Turin in 1880, he received a diploma, while at the one in 1989, he exhibited three hundred studies in a room specially reserved for him. He gave many of these to the city. Other examples of his work are in museums in Amsterdam, Florence, Montreal, Sydney, Nantes and Mulhouse.

Like Fromentin, with whom he was often compared, Pasini was struck by the delicacy of the light in the East. His treatment of the play between shadow and sun and his quasi-photographic representation of architecture and figures are a world apart from the imaginary exoticism of earlier Orientalist paintings. He excelled in group compositions of horses, their shiny rumps towards the spectator, held by simple soldiers who mix with merchants and passers-by. Small details are typical: dogs basking in the sun, a tree throwing its shadow onto a nearby wall. Pasini was particularly careful to study precise details of tilework and inscriptions, and in very many paintings, such as *Syrian Horsemen Paused at the Entrance to a Bazaar, Circassian Horsemen Awaiting their Leader, Khan Courtyard on a Market Day* and *Horse Market*, the architecture has an important place. Other pictures, of great charm, are of Turkish women. In veiled clusters, picnicking by a kiosk, relaxing in the garden of a country house, or holding parasols as they stroll through a busy street, they are reminiscent of the women found in the Turkish school of painting led by Osman Hamdy Bey. Silent, respectable, modest, they are a far cry from the slave girls, dancers and *femmes fatales* who served, in so many Orientalist paintings, to titillate the imagination of the Western public.

*Constantinople Market,* oil on canvas,
signed and dated 1874, 51.25 x 41.25 in
(130 x 105 cm). Private collection.

# Eugène
# PAVY

*French School*

*B*rother of Philippe Pavy, with whom he travelled in Tunisia, Algeria, Morocco, and perhaps Egypt, in the 1870s and 1880s. He exhibited his paintings of street merchants, armed sentries, palace guards and souks in both Paris and London, where he lived for a time. In London, from 1879 to 1884, he and his brother rented studios in Langham Chambers, just off Portland Place, a building which housed other artists as well as the Artists' Society. Pavy sent two Orientalist paintings to the Royal Academy, while eight works were shown at the Royal Society of British Artists and at the Grosvenor Gallery. Three others, acquired in 1898, are in the Glasgow Art Gallery.

*Market Day in Tangiers,* oil on panel, signed and dated Tanger 1885, 17.25 x 28.25 in (44 x 71.6 cm). Courtesy of the Mathaf Gallery, London.

*The Market Place*, oil on canvas, signed, 36 x 24 in (91.5 x 61 cm). Courtesy of the Mathaf Gallery, London.

146

# Philippe
## PAVY

**1860-**
*French School*

*The Guard of the Seraglio*, oil on panel, signed and dated 86, 18 x 12 in (45.8 x 30.5 cm). Private collection.

*B*oth Philippe Pavy and his brother Eugène specialised in paintings of North Africa and the Near East. They travelled together, and their work is indeed very similar. The Pavys lived in London for some time, and here Philippe showed his pictures, from 1874, at the Royal Society of British Artists, in Suffolk Street, and at the Royal Academy between 1874 and 1889. These included *Turkish Women at the Fountain* (1878), *A Circassian Slave* (1880), *A Jewel Merchant, Cairo* (1880) and *The Casbah, Algiers* (1882). Pavy probably went through Spain on his way to North Africa, for he painted scenes of Granada, Seville and Malaga. During the late 1880s, Pavy exhibited several times at the Société des Artistes Français, notably his fine painting entitled *Bride Arriving in a Village, Biskra, Algeria*. Generally painted on wood panels, the group compositions of Nubian soldiers, orange-vendors, chess-players, water-carriers, and processions are treated in a lively manner. They show an excellent balance between ethnographic detail and skilfully handled light values and harmonious colours.

*In the Bazaar,* oil on panel, signed
and dated 1878, 16.50 x 13.50 in
(42 x 34.3 cm). Courtesy of the Mathaf
Gallery, London.

# Henri
# REGNAULT

## Paris 1843-Buzenval 1871
### French School

*H*enri Regnault's patriotic death on the battlefield, which cut short his meteoric career, immortalized his name.

The son of Victor Regnault, a renowned research chemist and director of the porcelain manufactory at Sèvres, Regnault showed an early talent for drawing. With his inseparable friend Georges Clairin, he enrolled at Alexandre Cabanel's atelier at the Paris School of Fine Arts. Regnault always had to excell in everything, walking, swimming, hunting, riding and, of course, painting. He was therefore vexed and discouraged at twice failing to win the Prix de Rome. In 1866, he painted his competition piece *Thétis bringing to Achilles the Weapons forged by Vulcan* in a last-minute burst of energy, and at last won the Grand Prix.

During his stay in Rome, Regnault visited the studio of Mariano Fortuny y Marsal and was dazzled by his virtuosity and brilliant palette. The Spaniard's influence on his work did not make itself immediately felt, however; Regnault's first-year presentation picture, *Automedon* (Boston Museum of Fine Arts), with two superb fiery Arab horses, was in the pure Romantic tradition. One of the horses used as a model for this painting bolted with Regnault and threw him. Complications followed this accident and the artist went to Spain to recuperate. With Clairin, he enthusiastically studied Velásquez, sketched beggars, peasants, children, guards and soldiers, and, singing the *Marseillaise*, joined the rumpus in the streets as the Spanish population rose against Queen Isabella II. Regnault was commissioned by General Prim y Pratas to paint his triumphal entry into Madrid, but the general, who thoroughly disliked this brilliant equestrian portrait (Musée d'Orsay, Paris), later refused to accept it.

Regnault returned to Rome, but after the excitements of Spain, he found the city too exploited and overrun by foreigners and tourist guides. During this five-month stay, he painted his first work with an exotic background, *Judith and Holophernes* (Musée des Beaux-Arts, Marseilles) and began the outlines of *Salome*, which he called in turn *Herodias, African Woman, A Favorite Slave*, and *Córdoba Poetess*. Although penniless, he was determined to visit the Eastern world. The first step in this plan was to return to Spain with Clairin. The highlight of these months in late 1869 was Granada, with the Hispano-Moorish architecture of the Alhambra, which Regnault found overwhelmingly beautiful. He bought dozens of photographs and made numerous

*Salome*, oil on canvas, signed and dated Rome 1870, 63 x 40.50 in (160 x 102.9 cm). The Metropolitan Museum of Art, New York.

sketches of the inscriptions, the delicate stucco work and the azulejos, the last for his father, interested as always in ceramic techniques. In September, the young artist, unusually responsive and fervent, wrote to a friend: "Both Clairin and I are doomed to live brief lives. We lead too vagabond an existence, we take too many pains, we are consumed by too many ambitions and too many desires to endure for any great length of time. It is unlikely that the two of us will meet death together."

Regnault was at last able to go to Morocco at the end of the year, and rented a house with Clairin in Tangiers, which they decorated in the Oriental style. A seventeen-year-old Moroccan girl, Aïscha Chamma, was able to persuade Muslim women to sit for the two artists, but it was practically impossible for him to sketch people in the street. Regnault painted two rough sketches – *Interior in Tangiers* and *Moorish Gynaeceum* – took Arabic lessons, and finished *Salome*, which he sent back to Paris to be shown at the 1870 Salon. He was justifiably pleased with this canvas, with its striking colour contrasts that were most unusual for that time. The shimmering fabrics that gave the picture its exotic attraction had been bought by him at the Paris Universal Exhibition in 1867 and in Spain. He soon had plans for another important work. "My aim is to depict the real Moors in the way they used to be," he wrote, "rich and great, both terrifying and voluptuous, the ones that are to be found only in past history." He sent for an extra-large canvas from France and built himself a new studio on the outskirts of

Tangiers which gave him sufficient space to paint *A Summary Execution under the Moorish Kings of Granada* (Musée d'Orsay, Paris). In this spectacular picture, the harmony of the apricots, peaches and reds do nothing to mitigate the terrible violence of the bloody scene. When it was hung in the Musée du Luxembourg, people were said to be "so overcome by its horrible realism, as to be seized by faintness." Not all his work was so extreme and he painted more conventional pictures, such as *Departure for the Fantasia*, *Moroccan Sentry,* and *The Pasha's Outing, Tangiers.*

With the outbreak of the Franco-Prussian war, Regnault and Clairin hastened back to Paris to join the army, although as a pensioner of the French Academy in Rome, Regnault was exempt from military duty. In January 1871, he was killed during the battle of Buzenval. He had had time to complete only a few Orientalist pictures, but a retrospective exhibition held at the Paris School of Fine Arts in 1872 showed his varied subject matters, portraits, landscapes, costumes, animals and architecture. In April that year, one hundred and fifty oils, watercolours and drawings were auctioned, some of which were bought by the Musée du Luxembourg, by the comte de Louvencourt, by the baronne Nathaniel de Rothschild and by the baron Gustave de Rothschild.

*A Summary Execution under the Moorish Kings of Granada*, oil on canvas, signed and dated Tanger 1870, 118.75 x 57.50 in (302 x 146 cm). Musée d'Orsay, Paris.

Regnault
Tanger 1870

# David
# ROBERTS

## Stockbridge 1796-London 1864
### *Scottish School*

*"Under the Grand Portico"*,
watercolour and bodycolour, signed,
inscribed and dated Philae, Nov. 18th, 1838,
19 x 12.75 in (48.6 x 32.3 cm). Courtesy
of The Fine Art Society, London.

*D*avid Roberts was one of the first independent artists to visit the Near East. His journey, made amid conditions of discomfort, difficulty and danger, brought him fame and established him as one of the best-known painters of his day, both in Britain and on the Continent. Child of a humble family (his father was a shoemaker), Roberts was apprenticed for seven years to a house-painter in Edinburgh before earning his living as a scene-painter in the Scottish theatre. In 1822, he moved to London, working at Drury Lane and later at Covent Garden, and designing panoramas and dioramas. He found time, however, to paint for himself, and exhibited for the first time with the Society of British Artists in 1824. Once his work began to sell, he left the theatre forever, except for designing scenery for several of Charles Dickens' productions. At the end of 1832, Roberts went to Spain, attracted by the fact that this was a country whose architecture had so far been neglected by British painters. By the following spring, he was in Tangiers and Tetuan. Not only did his album of lithographic views of Spain make his reputation, but his adventures in Morocco whetted his appetite for further Eastern travel.

At this time, scholarly concern for the classical world was gradually being superseded by a growing interest in the ancient cultures of the Middle East, which were relevant to biblical history, and therefore of great interest to the Victorians. On the other hand, Islamic architecture, although it was beginning to attract attention in Europe, was still little known. It had long been Roberts' ambition to undertake this important and hazardous journey, and in 1838, he at last sailed for Alexandria. He spent several months sketching, writing letters and diaries, and exploring Upper Egypt and Nubia. The degree of desolation and solitude of these Egyptian ruins deeply impressed him, and, although feeling that he had perhaps not done them justice, he was immensely successful in communicating his

After eleven months' absence, Roberts returned home with hundreds of drawings and sketches. Like those of most topographical artists, these were drawn rapidly and decisively, but with sufficient detail to be used for prints or studio pictures. In addition, he possessed the rare gift of being able to paint from studies made many years earlier. From 1842 to 1849, his

*Suez*, handcoloured lithograph, dated Suez Feb. 11th 1839. Courtesy of the Mathaf Gallery, London.

sense of awe, particularly when he chose a low viewpoint to emphasize the superhuman scale of his subjects. The small groups of figures in the foreground only help to set off the grandeur of the monuments. In February 1839, he left for Sinai, Petra, Jaffa, Jerusalem (recently in quarantine during an outbreak of the plague), Nazareth, St. John of Acre, Tyre and Sidon, then on to Lebanon and Baalbek. Fever prevented him from including Damascus and Palmyra.

coloured prints, lithographed by Louis Haghe, were published in six volumes entitled *Views in the Holy Land, Syria, Idumea, Arabia, Egypt and Nubia*. These albums, many of which have been wantonly broken up, made his fortune, being the first records of the Holy Land to be presented to the British public. Roberts's experience as a theatre designer helped him to respond emotionally to the massive and dramatic ruins he had seen. He had a great talent for conveying the height and proportions of a building, achieving effects that can only be equalled in photography by using a

spot. Roberts's style of travel in the Near East had been magnificent, whether sailing up the Nile in a hired boat with a crew of eight, or crossing the desert in Arab costume, accompanied by a caravan of twenty-one camels and as many servants and Bedouin. Nothing quite ever matched up to this experience, and he never again ventured so far afield, confining his travels to Italy, France and Belgium, with visits to Scotland. Elected an associate member of the Royal Academy in 1839, then member in 1841, he painted Orientalist scenes until the end of his life.

wide-angled lens. This, and his instinct for balanced compositions with dramatic impact, make his watercolours and pencil and wash sketches of exceptional interest. He received many commissions for oil paintings based on his studies, but these often lack the freshness of his first impressions dashed off on the

*"The Ruins of the Temple of the Sun at Baalbec"*, oil on canvas, signed and dated 1842, 59 x 95 in (150 x 241 cm). Private collection.

*"Convent of St. Catherine with Mount Horeb"*, pencil, watercolour and bodycolour, signed, inscribed and dated Feb 19th 1839. Private collection.

# Charles
## ROBERTSON

**1844-Walton-on-Thames 1891**
*English School*

*The Sword Merchant,* oil on canvas,
signed with monogram and dated 1877,
15 x 9.50 in (38 x 24.5 cm). Courtesy of
the Mathaf Gallery, London.

*L*ike so many of his compatriots,
Charles Robertson was renowned
for his excellence in watercolours.
After studying in London, he spent
four years in Aix-en-Provence,
where he heard about the potentials
for young artists in Algeria, the
nearest of the French possessions.
He made a journey to North Africa
in 1862, at the age of eighteen, and
the following year, showed his first
Orientalist painting at the Royal
Academy. From then on, he made a
number of journeys, to the Italian
lakes in 1866 and 1867, Turkey and
the Holy Land in 1872, Egypt and
Tangiers in 1876. These were not
lightning tours, but were often
extended over a period of months or
sometimes years. His last trip was in
1889, to Egypt, Jerusalem,
Damascus, Turkey, Italy and Spain.
He intended to paint enough
watercolours to hold an important
exhibition but these, one hundred
and thirty in all, were shown at The
Fine Art Society in London only
after his early death.

Until 1880, Robertson painted
almost exclusively in oils, but from
1884, he worked only in
watercolour. He became so quickly
accomplished in this difficult
medium that he was elected member
of the Royal Watercolour Society.
He was also a regular contributor
to the Royal Academy and the New
Watercolour Society, becoming vice-
president of the Royal Society of
Painters and Etchers.

Robertson's work, colourful,
detailed, often dated, included such

titles as *A Khan in Damascus,
A Fruit Shop, Tangiers, The Mount
of Olives from Jerusalem, The Shoes
of the Faithful* and *Melon Seller,
Cairo.* Although these are of
everyday street scenes and
landscapes seen on his journeys, he
painted several imaginary works,
such as *The Grieving Pasha,* taken
from Victor Hugo's *Les Orientales,*
and *Sinbad in the Valley of
Diamonds,* from *The Thousand and
One Nights.*

*The Storyteller, Morocco,* watercolour,
signed with monogram and dated 1883,
23.50 x 50.75 in (60 x 129 cm).
Courtesy of the Mathaf Gallery, London.

*"A Carpet Sale, Cairo",* watercolour,
signed, 31 x 53 in (78.7 x 134.5 cm).
Courtesy of the Mathaf Gallery, London.

# Giulio
# ROSATI

**Rome 1858- 1917**
*Italian School*

*A*lthough of a family more inclined towards military and banking careers than the arts, Rosati nevertheless received his training at the Academia di San Luca. He soon became tired of the academic discipline and so left his professors, Dario Queric and Frencesco Podesti, in order to become a pupil of the popular Spanish painter, Luis Alvarez Catala. Rosati became one of the most prolific Orientalist artists of his time, painting numerous watercolours which emphasized the nobility of the Muslim culture. However, he had never undertaken a journey to the Maghreb and his information was entirely based on photographs, engravings and oriental objects, available in Rome. He rarely took part in exhibitions, preferring to sell his paintings directly to a picture dealer; many of his works were acquired by English, French and American collectors. Alberto Rosati, his son, painted in a similar style, but was less productive.

*Playing Backgammon,* watercolour, signed, 14 x 21 in (35.5 x 53.4 cm). Courtesy of the Mathaf Gallery, London.

*The Encampment,* watercolour, signed, 20.75 x 13.75 in (52.5 x 35 cm). Courtesy of the Mathaf Gallery, London.

*The Carpet Merchant*, watercolour, signed, 18 x 23 in (45.7 x 58.5 cm). Courtesy of the Mathaf Gallery, London.

# Adolf
## SCHREYER

**Frankfurt-am-Main 1828-Kronberg 1899**
*German School*

*A Mounted Arab Warrior,* oil on canvas,
signed, 32.50 x 27 in (82.5 x 69 cm).
Private collection.

$A$dolf Schreyer, a specialist in riders and horses in rural settings, both in Eastern Europe and North Africa, was enormously popular with the German aristocracy, as well as with millionaire American collectors such as Vanderbilt, Astor, Rockefeller and Morgan.

After studying in Frankfurt, Stuttgart, Munich and Düsseldorf (his lessons including riding and equine anatomy), Schreyer travelled with Prince Thurn and Taxis in 1848 or 1849 through Hungary, Wallachia and southern Russia. In 1855, he followed the regiment commanded by the prince as an artist-reporter assigned to cover the Crimean war. He did not go to the Crimea itself, however, but to the eastern reaches of the Danube, the Austrian army's field of action in the conflict. He visited Syria and Egypt in 1856 or 1859, and Algiers in 1861, mastering several Arab dialects and thoroughly immersing himself in Bedouin life. He settled in Paris until the outbreak of the Franco-Prussian war obliged him to leave. He then went to live in Kronberg, but occasionally returned to Paris. Schreyer was the court painter to the Grand Duke of Mecklenburg, exhibited at the Paris Salon and in other European cities, and held membership in the Amsterdam and Rotterdam Academies. A number of German and American museums own examples of his work.

Throughout his thirty-year-long career, Schreyer continued to paint snowy scenes of Wallachian, Moldavian and Russian peasants or soldiers and their horses, which he had seen in his youth. These were as much appreciated as his pictures of Algerian horsemen. Schreyer first showed the latter in violent action, but later painted them riding their way quietly over rough ground, alone or in small groups. The choice of subject matter is clearly inspired by Fromentin (some of the copies made at the time of Schreyer's pictures even bear Fromentin's name), but his figures are generally in close-up, not in the middle distance as is usually the case in Fromentin's pictures. The colour schemes are characteristic; white and red clothing, red bridles and harnesses, a pale blue sky filled with puffy clouds, and a brown, rust and ochre ground. At their best, Schreyer's pictures are painted with real verve and brio, at their worst, they are rather heavy repetitions of stock themes.

*Mounted Bedouin,* oil on panel, signed,
27 x 39.50 in (68.5 x 100.5 cm).
Private collection.

# Thomas
# SEDDON

## London 1821-Cairo 1856
*English School*

*Portrait of Richard Burton in Arab Dress,*
watercolour, signed and dated 1854,
11 x 8 in (28.2 x 20 cm). Courtesy of The
Fine Art Society, London.

*T*homas Seddon was closely associated with the Pre-Raphaelite painters, and the few pictures he painted of the Near East before his untimely death belong more in feeling and technique to this group than to the mainstream Orientalists. The son of a well-known furniture maker, he visited Paris, Barbizon and the Brittany sea town of Dinan, before first exhibiting at the Royal Academy in 1852. He left for Cairo at the end of 1853, where he met Edward Lear, whose "advice as an experienced traveller," he said, "has been very useful." He also came across Richard Burton, a linguist and Arab scholar who, brilliant and intolerant of convention and restraint, was one of the most fascinating people of his time. Seddon painted Burton in full Arab costume; this portrait was used in lithographic form to illustrate the English explorer's account of his daring and risky journey to Mecca, *Personal Narrative of a Pilgrim to Al-Madinah & Meccah*, published in 1855. After the watercolour version was exhibited in London by The Fine Art Society in 1978, the same portrait in oil, left by Seddon in Egypt, turned up in a private collection.

In the spring of 1854, Seddon left Cairo for Palestine in the company of Holman Hunt. This was partly to study the Pre-Raphaelite's technical mastery, and partly to avoid going back to work in his father's business. While he lacked Hunt's high-minded reasons for visiting the Holy Land, Seddon, by painting biblical landscapes, was atoning for (according to his brother) "a taste for pleasure and dissipation which he had formed in Paris." It was on this journey that Hunt painted his famous symbolic picture, *The Scapegoat*, at which he worked away in the blazing sun while repulsing attacks from hostile Arab tribesmen. Seddon arrived back in Dinan in November 1854 and set about organising a private exhibition of his works in London for the following year. These were highly praised by the theorist John Ruskin, who raised a fund after Seddon's death to offer his key painting, *Jerusalem and the Valley of Jehoshaphat from the Hill of Evil Counsel* to the nation. A watercolour repetition of this

*Esbekeeyah, Cairo*. He returned to Cairo in the same year but, already in fragile health from rheumatic fever, fell ill and died. An exhibition of his works was held at the Society of Arts in London in 1857, on which occasion Ruskin gave a speech saying that although Seddon might have outgrown his "careful, faithful, conscientious and poetical" technique, he was, owing to his early death, "the purest Pre-Raphaelite landscape painter."

composition, in the Ashmolean museum, Oxford, was painted directly over a photograph, either of the landscape itself or of the oil painting. In 1856, Seddon showed pictures at the Royal Academy, including *An Arab Sheikh and Tents in the Egyptian Desert* and *Interior of a Deewan, formerly belonging to the Copt Patriarch near the*

*"Dromedary and Arabs at the City of the Dead, with the Tomb of Sultan El Barkook in the Background"*, oil on canvas, signed and dated Egypt 1854, 11 x 14 in (28 x 35.5 cm). Courtesy of The Fine Art Society, London.

# Giuseppe
# SIGNORINI

## Rome 1857-Rome 1932
*Italian School*

*Warrior with a Red Hat,* watercolour,
signed and inscribed Roma,
26.75 x 16.50 in (68 x 42 cm).
Courtesy of Alain Lesieutre, Paris.

*I*n 1889, Signorini joined the
Scuola di Geometria of the
Academia di San Luca in Rome, his
home city. He later became a pupil
of the Roman painter Aurelio
Tiratelli, who introduced him to all
the foremost Italian artists of the
time. He became increasingly
interested in Salon painting and
made frequent visits to Paris, where
he could admire the works of the
Spanish Orientalist Mariano Fortuny
y Marsal, Ernest Meissonier and
Jean-Léon Gérôme. From 1899 until
his death, Signorini owned two
studios, one in Rome, the other in
Paris, dividing his time between the
two capitals. A brilliant
watercolourist, much in demand by
European and American collectors,
he specialised in portraits, then in
elegant people in 18th century
costume, jovial cardinals and
dashing musketeers, but also in the
inhabitants of the Maghreb and the
Near East. In the 1880s, Signorini
played an important part in the
popularization of themes based
on the Muslim world and he himself
owned an important collection
of Islamic works of art and textiles.
After his death, his work was much
admired, and exhibitions were held
in Milan in 1949 and 1950, and in
Turin in 1946 and 1970.

*Market*, watercolour, signed and inscribed
Roma, 5.75 x 8.75 in (14.4 x 22 cm).
Courtesy of the Mathaf Gallery, London.

*Cairo Market Scene*, oil on canvas,
signed and inscribed Cairo,
23 x 34 in (58.4 x 86.4 cm). Courtesy of
the Mathaf Gallery, London.

# Robert
# TALBOT KELLY

**Birkenhead 1861-London 1934**
*English School*

**A** son of the Dublin-born landscape painter Robert George Kelly, he grew up in a large family. Although he left school early, in 1876, to take up employment in a Liverpool cotton-brokers' firm, his parents encouraged his talents for painting and music. He studied with his father and exhibited his first pictures under the name of R.G. Kelly, Jnr. In the early 1880s, he was sent on a cruise by his employers to recover from a period of overwork. This journey marked a turning point in his life. He resigned from his job, adopted the old family name of Talbot (to avoid confusion with his father's name; later on, he was sometimes referred to as Talbot-Kelly). He visited North Africa, and settled in Egypt, which became his

*Caravan,* watercolour, signed and dated 1893, 11 x 21.50 in (28 x 54.5 cm).
Courtesy of the Mathaf Gallery, London.

second country. He owned a studio in Cairo and became fluent in Arabic; for a while, he lived with the Bedouin. Although he spent some years in England after his marriage, most of his career was spent in Egypt until 1915. By 1902, when he published his book *Egypt Painted* and Described by R. Talbot Kelly, illustrated with his own pictures, his reputation as an artist and traveller had been established. In Cairo, he received commissions from dignitaries and members of the aristocracy who visited his studio as part of their tour of Egypt. He was a member of the Royal Society of British Artists, the Royal Institute of Painters in Watercolours and the Royal British Colonial Society of Artists. In 1903-4, he visited Burma at the request of the

light and oppressive heat, he emphasized the relationship between man and the relentless desert. One of his major works, *The Flight of the Khalifa after his Defeat at the Battle of Omdurman*, is in the collection of the Walker Art Gallery in Liverpool, while the Williamson Art Gallery in Birkenhead owns such watercolours as *Eastern Lake* (1892), *On the Nile* (1903), *A Nile Village* (1911), and *The Hunter* (1912).

government. Talbot Kelly was above all an excellent watercolourist, who depended on subtly graduated tints – pink, pale yellow, buff and eggshell blue – for his atmospheric effects. In his paintings of solitary riders surrounded by sandy wastes, or of Bedouin marching in harsh

*In the Mosque*, Cairo, watercolour, signed and dated 1897. Courtesy of the Mathaf Gallery, London.

# Charles-Emile
# VACHER DE TOURNEMINE

## Toulon 1812-Toulon 1872
### *French School*

*C*harles Vacher de Tournemine's Orientalist paintings are typical of the majority exhibited at the Paris Salons during the 1850s and 1860s; pleasant genre scenes in rich tones which pleased the public, but exasperated many critics.

"Everybody off in his own little corner has set about 'doing' the Eastern world and its colours," Lagenvais wrote. Certainly, many of these "neo-colourists," as they were dubbed, painted scenes of the Middle East without ever having set foot there. Vacher de Tournemine, however, was a great traveller. Service in the navy between 1825 and 1831 brought him in contact with countries around the Mediterranean. He took part in the battle of Navarino and the seizing of Algiers. He then visited the Balearic Isles, Asia Minor, Cyprus, Lebanon and Egypt. After nine years' further service, this time in the army, he left to study painting in Paris in Isabey's studio. In 1846, Vacher de Tournemine began to exhibit at the Salon, showing scenes brought back from a long stay in Brittany, but after 1852, his paintings were almost exclusively Orientalist. Many of these were variations on his favourite theme: peaceful villages or small houses on the water's edge, the azure sky and white and ochre walls set off by the red and turquoise clothes of the small figures. Of these, the best known is his *Turkish Dwellings near Adalia, Asia Minor*, now in the Louvre museum.

Other journeys followed, Algeria and Tunisia in 1853, the Danube and the Balkans in 1860 and, in 1863, Asia Minor, where he explored areas both dangerous and little-visited.

During his stay in Adramitti, he witnessed a procession such as the one he describes here: "Imagine a Turkish wedding procession," he wrote in a letter dated July 1863. "A group of *zeibecks* lead the way, bearing red and yellow poles from which flutter the bride's shawls and scarves. They are followed by three individuals beating on big drums, accompanied by flute music sharp enough to pierce your ears and make you take to your heels. Next comes the bridegroom with all his friends. From time to time the procession comes to a halt, and one of its members carries a small sugarloaf into a house: this constitutes an invitation to the wedding feast. Then the burlesque dancing resumes with renewed frenzy."

His last trip was to Egypt in 1869, for the opening of the Suez Canal. Although he exhibited pictures of India from 1868, temples, hunting scenes, festivals, these were painted from imagination; he never actually went there.

The founder of a well-known revue, *Les Artistes Contemporains*, which disseminated French art in Europe, Vacher de Tournemine was attached during the Commune to the Musée

de Tournemine was popular with foreign collectors, for, according to the catalogue of the posthumous studio sale in 1873, his paintings were already rare and few were to be found in France.

There has always been a certain amount of confusion in biographical notes about his name. Although the artist signed his work Ch. de Tournemine, he was in fact the natural son of Bernard Vacher de Tournemine, although declared at birth as Tournemire.

du Luxembourg, which housed paintings by living artists. Here, he had the responsibility of saving the collections from harm. He was later named assistant curator. He had for some time been on the administrative lists, and five of his paintings in nine years were bought by the State at fairly high prices. Several were sent to provincial museums, Montpellier, Toulon and Marseilles. It seems that Vacher

*Houses on the Edge of the Water, Asia Minor,* oil on panel, signed, 21.50 x 39.25 in (55 x 100 cm). Private collection.

# Horace
## VERNET

### Paris 1789-Paris 1863
*French School*

*H*orace Vernet was probably the most adulated of the nineteenth-century French military painters. Born with a silver spoon in his mouth – literally, in the Palais du Louvre – he was soon to gain fame and fortune. He came from a celebrated family of artists: his father, Carle Vernet, was a painter of horses and battle scenes, and his grand-father, Joseph Vernet, specialized in seascapes. Horace, the last of this Vernet "dynasty," found every door open to him. He won a first-class medal at twenty-two, became a Chevalier of the Legion of Honour at twenty-five, a member of the Institut at thirty-six and the director of the French Academy in Rome at thirty-eight. Although the Vernets were traditionally royalist, Horace rallied to Napoleon, then sided with the liberals under the Bourbon Restoration (although this did not prevent him from obtaining an official commission from King Charles X). The revolution of 1830 brought his protector and personal friend, King Louis-Philippe, to the throne, which greatly helped his career. Later, he briefly rallied to the republic after the events of 1848, but then found himself the official painter of the Second Empire. An opportunist? A political turncoat ? He certainly had an extraordinary ability to adapt to the various regimes, while remaining highly successful.

The young Vernet had totally participated in the Romantic movement. He painted, with energy and exuberance, vibrantly coloured battle scenes, both medieval and modern, poetic fables, the frenzy of wild horses and themes inspired by such writers as Lord Byron and Victor Hugo: *Mazeppa* (1825) and *Giaour* (1827). But the painter of these dramatic and turbulent battles, so admired by Stendhal at the 1824 Salon, began to change his style after his appointment as director of the French Academy in Rome in 1828. Vernet made the first of many journeys to Algeria in 1833, in the company of the English artist William Wyld. He felt that Africa was the land of the future – "a gold mine for France" – and later became the owner of a considerable amount of property at Ben Koula. Convinced that the gestures and attitudes of the Arabs had been identical for thousands of years, and that he was witnessing living scenes from the Bible, he began to paint religious pictures interpreted through the lives of contemporary nomads. Beginning with the *Arab Storyteller*, painted for the twelfth Earl of Pembroke in 1833, he abandoned the ardour and fluidity of the Romantic style to paint Orientalist and biblical scenes with sharp precision and great ethnographical detail. This practice of clothing biblical figures in modern Arab costume – *Hagar repudiated by Abraham,* (1837, Musée des Beaux-Arts, Nantes), *Judah and Tamar,* (1840, Wallace Collection, London), *Joseph's Coat* (1853) shocked the public and he was obliged to defend his ideas before the Academy, with evidence gathered during his travels. In 1848, he published an article in *L'Illustration* on the comparisons between the costume of the Ancient Hebrews and that of modern Arabs. In 1835, Vernet was replaced in Rome by Ingres and returned to France just after King Louis-Philippe had created a museum of military history in Versailles. Vernet was

panoramic canvases were novel in so far as there was no longer a central hero, as was the tradition; even the humblest infantryman played his part in the giant compositions, packed with little incidents which were of equal value. Exhibited at the 1845 Salon, the *Smalah* drew enormous crowds – and adverse critical opinions, including the following: "It's a whole novel... but composed of a

commissioned to decorate one of the principal galleries, for which he painted episodes from the conquest of Algeria, *The Siege of Constantine, Battle of the Habrah* and the famous *Capture of Abd el-Kader's Retinue*, which measures a staggering 21.39 metres long! Vernet's

*The Battle of Isly,* oil on canvas, signed, 19.25 x 23.50 in (49 x 60 cm). Private collection.

series of installments," and "The battle-scene painters are transforming themselves into news reporters."

His journeys – many to Algeria, and to Morocco, Egypt, Syria, Palestine, Turkey and the Crimea – were not always made in great style. Indeed, he took any means of transport available, boat, wagon, sledge, horse, camel, mule, camping in tents or even in the open air. Vernet, a blend of adventurer and official artist, had a large production (some 500 paintings and 200 lithographs, according to the writer Lagrange).

*Joseph's Coat*, oil on canvas, shaped top, signed and dated Afrique 1853, 55 x 41 in (140 x 104 cm). Wallace Collection, London.

As a professor at the Paris School of Fine Arts, he had an enormous influence on the artistic organizations of his time, on juries, Salons and competitions. He also received many commissions from the State, the grand bourgeoisie and high-ranking army officers. His lithographed sketches and paintings, published on a large scale, earned him immense public renown. He was, however, ferociously attacked both personally and professionally, not only during his lifetime but posthumously.

*The Lion Hunt,* oil on canvas, signed and dated 1836, 22.50 x 32.25 in (57 x 82 cm). Wallace Collection, London.

# Émile
## Vernet-Lecomte

**Paris 1821-Paris 1900**
*French School*

*T*here has always been a certain amount of confusion about the name of this artist, whose striking paintings have been shown in a number of recent European and American exhibitions. The son of the military painter Hippolyte Lecomte, who married Camille, daughter of the famous artist Carle Vernet, Émile Lecomte was therefore a nephew of the painter Horace Vernet. He studied with his uncle before initially showing at the Salon in 1843 under the name of Émile Lecomte. He later took the name of Vernet-Lecomte, with which he signed his paintings. The Salon catalogues, however, often inaccurate from the point of view of spelling, incorrectly listed his name for many years as Lecomte-Vernet before later inverting it. This error has been repeated by many of the art dictionaries, as has the erroneous 1874 death date.

Vernet-Lecomte painted a wide variety of subjects, including society portraits, religious paintings (many commissioned to decorate Paris churches and administration buildings) and pictures devoted to Orientalist themes. The first of these, *Portrait of a Syrian Man* and *Syrian Woman,* were shown at the 1847 Salon. Often featuring bold single figures of great beauty, they included *Syrian Girl playing with a Panther* (1850), *Fellaheen Woman carrying her Child, Egypt* (1864), *Dancing Woman, Egypt* (1866), and *Maronite Girl, Asia Minor* (1867). He also exhibited episodes of the siege of Sebastopol and the French expedition to Syria of 1860 after the massacre of Christians by the Druses. Although there are no details of his journeys, it seems more than likely that he actually travelled: an oil, painted in Cairo in 1863, and signed Émile Lecomte, shows a European artist sitting under a great tree while he sketches an encampment.

*Berber Woman,* oil on canvas, signed and dated 1870, 48 x 34.50 in (122 x 87 cm). Private collection.

# Georges
## WASHINGTON

**Marseilles 1827-Douarnenez 1901**
*French School*

*The Standard Bearer*, oil on canvas,
signed, 28.75 x 23.50 in (73 x 60 cm).
Courtesy of Alain Lesieutre, Paris.

*A*n illegitimate child, Washington was declared at birth under the name of the American hero so admired by his father. He was brought up by his aunt, who wanted him to join her in the family business, but Washington was little attracted to trade. Passionately fond of painting, he became the pupil of François-Edouard Picot. But he found this conventional fine arts teaching stifling and so undertook a journey to Algeria. On his return to Paris, he married Léonie, daughter of the history painter Félix Philippoteaux. In 1879, Washington left for Morocco to make sufficient studies in order to carry out a Panorama of Tetuan for which he had received a commission. Another order from the same Belgian firm led him to travel through Hungary, Bulgaria, Turkey, Armenia and Caucasia. Once his enormous paintings were finished,

Washington accompanied them to Moscow in 1881, where they were shown to a paying public. In Paris, he entrusted dealers such as Durand-Ruel and Bernheim to sell his Orientalist pictures.

In 1884, endowed with the legacy he received on the death of Philippoteaux, Washington put a good many of his works up for auction at Drouot and, with his wife, launched into farming in Brittany. This proved disasterous and, finding himself in a desperate financial situation, left in 1888 for New York where he had once again received a commission for a Panorama. Even though he sold his pictures well on the spot, he returned to France to face bankrupcy. Installed in a small studio in Montmartre, he endlessly painted scenes of Algerian horsemen from memory. He spent his last years of his life in Douarnenez, in Brittany, with his daughter and son-in-law.

*Riders' Halt,* oil on canvas, signed, 28.50 x 37.25 in (72.5 x 95 cm).
Courtesy of the Gallery Keops, Geneva.

# Rudolf
# WEISSE

## Usti, Bohemia 1869-
### Swiss School

**W**eisse, pupil of the Akademie der Bildenden Kunst in Vienna, took part from time to time at the Paris Salon of the Société des Artistes Français between 1889 and 1927. He was awarded a medal at the 1889 Universal Exhibition for two paintings shown in the Austro-Hungarian section: *After the War – Oriental scene* and *Portrait of a Woman*; in 1920, he won a gold medal in Vienna. Weisse's Orientalist paintings show above all the daily life in Cairo, in a meticulous academic style very close to that of the Austrian artists, Ludwig Deutsch and Rudolf Ernst, who also lived in Paris. Weiss should not be confused with his homonym, the Swiss artist Rudolf Weisse, born in 1846, who travelled in the Ottoman Empire.

*The Vendor of Eastern Curios,* oil on
panel, signed and dated 87,
23.25 x 19 in (59 x 48.2 cm).
Courtesy of the Mathaf Gallery, London.

*Praying in the Mosque,* oil on panel, signed and dated Paris 86, 24 x 19.25 in (61 x 49 cm). Courtesy of the Mathaf Gallery, London.

# Carl
# WERNER

Weimar 1808-Leipzig 1894
*German School*

*The Entrance to the Bazaar,* watercolour, signed and dated 1863, 19.75 x 13.75 in (50 x 35 cm). Courtesy of the Mathaf Gallery, London.

*C*arl Werner was a pupil at the Leipzig Academy of Schnorr von Carolsfeld, a history painter linked with the Nazarene group of artists. In 1829, he went on to study architecture in Munich, but returned to painting two years later. Having won a travelling scholarship, he went to Italy, where he lived for nearly twenty years. Werner became known as one of the leading European watercolourists, and established a teaching atelier in Venice.

Besides his frequent trips to England, he toured Spain in 1856-57, followed by an extensive journey to Egypt and Palestine between 1862 and 1864. His *Carl Werner's Nile Sketches*, published in 1875, contained watercolours done during that time. He made some splendid watercolours in Jerusalem, particularly of the Dome of the Rock. He painted the outside of the sanctuary from nearby, unlike most travellers, who showed it from a distance, as part of a general view of Jerusalem. He was also able to paint the inside, a rare event, for this sacred shrine had always been difficult of access to non-Muslims. A member of the Venice and Leipzig Academies (he became a professor at the latter institution), Werner showed his work in Italy, Germany and England, particularly at the New Watercolour Society in London. His pictures, which included such titles as *View of Beirut, Isle of Philae, Mosque at Damascus, The Jordan near Jericho* and *Gate of Justice at Cairo,* are to be found in many European museums. Werner made further trips, to Greece and Sicily and in 1891, at the age of eighty-three, he returned to Rome and then to Leipzig, where he died.

*The Holy Rock, Jerusalem,* watercolour,
signed and dated 1866, 13.75 x 19.75 in
(35 x 50.2 cm). Courtesy of the Mathaf
Gallery, London.

*View of Jerusalem,* watercolour, signed and
dated 1864, 12 x 21 in (30.5 x 53.5 cm).
Courtesy of the Mathaf Gallery, London.

# Charles
# WILDA

---

### Vienna 1854-Vienna 1907
*Austrian School*

Wilda studied at the Vienna
Academy of Fine Art under Leopold
Carl Müller, who exerted a
considerable influence on his pupils.
He not only encouraged them to
travel to Egypt, but instilled high
standards of academic painting.
During the 1880s, Wilda visited
Cairo, where he had a studio. Like
his compatriots Swoboda and Kosler,
he sold his paintings to travellers,
particularly English visitors
wintering in Egypt. Indeed, so great
was the demand for this type
of painting that Müller encouraged
his pupils to go on with it, as they
were certain of making a good
living. Wilda shared a studio in Paris
with his friend Arthur von Ferraris
and, in 1889, the two artists showed
paintings of Cairo mosques
at the Salon de la Société des
Artistes Français. Participator in the
Austrian section at the 1900
Universal Exhibition, Wilda won a
gold medal for his *Arab Prophet.*

*The Fortune-Teller,* oil on canvas,
signed and dated Cairo 1894, 23 x 32 in
(58.5 x 81.3 cm). Courtesy of the Mathaf
Gallery, London.

Besides his portrayals of artisans at
work or merchants hawking their
wares, he painted more architectural
scenes, such as *Forecourt of a
Mosque, Cairo* and *Entrance to the*

*Aqala'un-el-Elfi Mosque, Cairo.*
Other pictures include *Arab
Soothsayer*, for which he received
the Kaiserpreis in 1895, and
*Washerwomen on the Nile.*

*At the Water's Edge,* oil on canvas,
signed and dated 1897, 36 x 26.50 in
(91.5 x 67.4 cm). Courtesy of the Mathaf
Gallery, London.

# William
## WYLD

**London 1806-Paris 1889**
*English School*

*Bab Azoun Street, Algiers*, watercolour,
signed, 28 x 17 in (71 x 43.3 cm).
Courtesy of the Mathaf Gallery, London.

**W**illiam Wyld visited Algiers only three years after it had been taken by the French in 1830. But unlike the official artists who accompanied the army, he was interested not in military exploits, but in intimate scenes of cafés, souks, streets and the port. Wyld, who hailed from a family of London merchants, launched on a diplomatic career at a very young age, being averse to the commercial world. He spent four years as a secretary to the English consul in Calais, where he took lessons in watercolour painting from Louis Francia. On the death of his father, he was obliged to give up his career, and became an agent in champagne for an English company in Epernay. It was during these six years that he studied oil painting. In 1833, he accompanied Horace Vernet, with whom he was already acquainted, to Algiers, and, later, to Spain and Italy. In Rome, Wyld quickly found purchasers for his work. Not only did Vernet have many connections as the director of the French Academy, he held salons every Thursday to entertain artists, French visitors and important people. In 1835, Wyld published an illustrated album, *Voyage Pittoresque dans la Régence d'Alger exécuté en 1833*, with plates lithographed by himself and Emile Lessore. He dedicated this album to Vernet. He later brought out another album, this time with views of Paris (1839).

Like his close friend Richard Parkes Bonington, Wyld was above all a brilliant watercolourist. He exhibited at the Paris Salon from 1839 and, from 1848, showed his work in England, at the New Watercolour Society, the Royal Academy and the British Institution. He was elected member of the Royal Institute of Painters in Watercolour in 1879. His work was soon much appreciated in England, particularly by great merchants and rich industrialists from the Midlands. At the 1855 Universal Exhibition in Paris, Wyld was included in the French School category, at the request of the comte de Nieuwerkerke, the Superintendent of Fine Arts. He was also awarded the Legion of Honour in recognition of the important part that he had played in encouraging French watercolour painting.

*Algiers Harbour*, watercolour, signed and dated 1833, 18 x 25 in (45.6 x 63.5 cm). Courtesy of the Mathaf Gallery, London.

# Félix
## ZIEM

### Beaune 1821-Paris 1911
*French School*

*Encampment,* oil on canvas, signed,
35 x 45.50 in (89 x 116 cm).
Courtesy of the Galerie du Léthé, Paris.

*F*élix Ziem's name is indissociable from the two sources of his inspiration, Venice and Constantinople. Enormously admired in his lifetime, he was judged harshly for years after his death, mainly because of the vulgarity of much of his large production. Only recently have his almost abstract studies of pure colour and his more personal paintings been isolated from the commercial mass and appreciated at their just value. From a simple family – his Polish father was a tailor – Ziem swiftly ascended the social ladder. While working as a construction foreman in Marseilles, he showed his watercolours to the duc d'Orléans, who had just returned from the Portes de Fer expedition in Algeria. Commissions soon followed. In 1843, he went to Russia with Prince Grigori Gagarin, himself an artist, and, during this stay of nearly two years, gave lessons to the grand duchesses in St. Petersburg. He made several journeys to Algeria, Tunisia, Morocco, Egypt and Asia Minor. He probably visited Turkey for the first time around 1848, returning in 1856 on a trip to Constantinople, Beirut and Cairo. He made frequent journeys to Italy as well: "The Eastern world," he said, "also includes Venice." He read and spoke Arabic and built his studio in Martigues in the Oriental style. Although he painted during seventy years, Ziem only sent his views of Venice and the Orient to the Salons from 1849 to 1868, and again after 1888. Few artists have known such success and he was covered with honours. The large pictures considered typical of Ziem, which were painted in his studio, showed a Venice and a Constantinople untouched by modern civilisation. His eternally repeated themes – the lagoon, the Golden Horn, caïques on the Bosphorus, fantasias, sultanas and harems – were mere displays of colour, unnatural pinks, yellows and azure blues. It is his oil sketches and watercolours that are the most diverse and personal. Painted outdoors, they show Ziem's interest in the scenes of everyday life in the East, crowded streets, souks, artisans, vendors and sundry ethnic types. In time, these preparatory sketches, became increasingly looser until there was no preliminary drawing, only dabs, squiggles and trails of pure colour which suggested the subject more than they defined it. Unlike his finished paintings, the watercolours were often dated, and sometimes even displayed the hour. Ziem loved to fabulize, which led press articles released before his death being filled with misleading information. His work was widely copied, with forged signatures, while the names on his followers' paintings were sometimes removed and replaced with Ziem's name by unscrupulous owners. In 1905, Ziem donated around one hundred works to the Paris Musée du Petit Palais. In 1912, a large part of his œuvre, left in his studio after his death, was given by his widow to the museums of Beaune, Dijon and Marseilles and to the Ziem museum in Martigues.

*Busy Street in Syria*, oil on panel, signed, 19 x 11.25 in (48.5 x 28.5 cm). Private collection.

# INDEX

# ACKNOWLEDGMENTS

Numerous museum curators and staff, auctioneers, art historians and experts, dealers, collectors, university students, as well as artists and artists' families, have provided information and photographs. We would like to express our thanks to Gerald M. Ackerman, Maîtres Ader Tajan, Lucien Arcache, Louise d'Argencourt, Artus et Associés, Albert Benamou, Koudir Benchikou, Petra Bopp, Rodney Brangwyn, Maître Eric Buffetaud, David B. Chalmers, Edmonde Charles-Roux, Michael Conforti (Director of the Clark Art Institute), Maîtres Couturier et de Nicolaÿ, François Daulte, Marie-Christine David, Jean de la Hogue, Fouad Debbas, Marie-Colette Depierre, Dominique Durand, George Encil, The Fine Art Society, Ilene Susan Fort, Galerie Antinéa, Galerie Arlette Gimaray, Galerie Félix Marcilhac, Galerie Intemporel, Galerie Jonas, Galerie du Léthé, Galerie Nataf, Galerie Resche, Maîtres Gros et Delettrez, Philippe Grunchec, Avner Gruszow, William R. Johnston (Walters Art Gallery, Baltimore), Jordan National Museum of Fine Arts, Amman, Marie and Guy Joubert, Caroline Juler, Geneviève Lacambre (Musée d'Orsay, Paris), Amélie Lefébure (Musée Condé, Chantilly), Jean-Claude Lesage, Briony Llewellyn, Rachel Liberman, Brian MacDermot (Mathaf Gallery), Henri Marchal, Djillali Mehri, Meissirel Fine Art, Danièle Menu, Dewey F. Mosby (The Colgate University Art Collections, Hamilton, New York), Didier Ottinger, Roberto Perazonne, Véronique Prat, Richard Green Galleries, Dr. Donald Rosenthal (Memorial Art Gallery, University of Rochester, New York), Kurt E. Schon, Ltd., Arlette Serullaz (Musée du Louvre and Musée Delacroix, Paris), Véronique Sisman, Jean-Roger Soubiran, Jean Soustiel, MaryAnne Stevens, D. Dodge Thompson (National Gallery of Art, Washington), James Thompson, Jean Trombert, The Victoria and Albert Museum, London, Françoise Zafrani, as well as to private collectors who wish to remain anonymous.

# PHOTOGRAPHIC CREDITS

DR, A.C.R., Lynne Thornton, Mes. Ader Tajan (Paris), Mes. Couturier et Nicolaÿ (Paris), Christie's (New York), Finarte (Milan), The Fine Art Society (London), Galerie Antinéa (Paris), Galerie Arlette Gimaray (Paris), Galerie du Léthé (Paris), Gallery Keops (Geneva), Mes. Gros et Delettrez (Paris), Alain Lesieutre (Paris), Mathaf Gallery (London), Meissirel Fine Art (Paris), Sotheby's (London, New York, Paris) and Chaline, Paul, Carpentras, p. 120 ; Danvers, Alain, Bordeaux, p. 55 ; Fotostudio Otto, Vienna, p. 141 ; Kleinhempel, Ralph, Hamburg, p. 13 ; Kopp, Michel, Geneva, pp. 73, 156 ; Photo Alix, Bagnères-de Bigorre, p. 121 ; Réunion des Musées Nationaux, Paris, pp. 42, 43, 45, 54, 56, 153.